1990

Animal Lifestyles and Anatomies

Animal Lifestyles

UNIVERSITY OF WASHINGTON PRESS

Seattle and London

and Anatomies

The Case of the Prosimian Primates

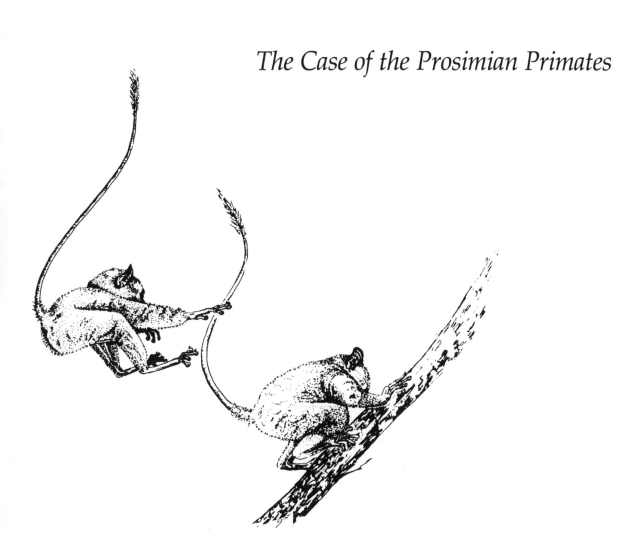

CHARLES E. OXNARD

ROBIN H. CROMPTON

SUSAN S. LIEBERMAN

Library of Congress Cataloging-in-Publication Data

Oxnard, Charles E., 1933–
    Animal lifestyles and anatomies : the case of the prosimian primates / Charles E.
Oxnard, Robin H. Crompton, and Susan S. Lieberman.
        p.   cm.
    Bibliography: p.
    Includes index.
    ISBN 0-295-096839-7
    1. Primates—Behavior. 2. Primates—Anatomy.   I. Crompton, Robin H.   II. Lie-
berman, Susan S.   III. Title.   IV Title: Prosimian primates.
    QL737.P9095   1989
    599.8'1'051—dc20   89-4875

Contents

Preface

One of the problems facing primate biologists is the association between anatomies and lifestyles: to what extent are the structures of animals related to their ways of life, and vice versa? Though detailed knowledge of primate anatomies has been available for many years, equivalent knowledge of primate lifestyles has been considerably more sketchy. This has become especially apparent as modern methods of investigating animal structures using mathematical, physical, and engineering techniques have provided better and better information about structural adaptations. In particular, the form and pattern of the primate skeleton have recently been explicated in a way more complete than ever before through the application of multivariate statistical analysis—morphometrics. This method of study has resulted in insights about anatomy that were unsuspected from prior studies.

But when it comes to the lifestyle side of the anatomy/lifestyle equation, it has always seemed that the best that could be done was to rely upon the locomotor classification. Yet we have always known that this reliance overly simplified the situation, being dependent, as it was, upon defining only the most obvious feature of a lifestyle. And we have also known that such classifications ignored not only many less obvious facets of lifestyles that animals display, but also those lifestyle features that they do not adopt.

It has long been my hope that an expansion of our understanding of primate lifestyles could come about through a mechanism similar to what we have applied to anatomies; that is, quantification of lifestyles, broadly defined, and analysis using multivariate statistical methods. This had always seemed a pipe dream until an unexpected collaboration with Robin Crompton, whose expertise is in field studies of prosimians, as well as in their functional anatomy, and with Susan Lieberman, whose academic background is in tropical ecology and evolution as well as quantitative biology, has allowed the dream to become reality.

The new studies outlined in this book are therefore aimed at understanding prosimian lifestyles, and the results of the lifestyle studies are then compared with equivalent quantitative studies of prosimian anatomies that have already been prosecuted. We have chosen to study prosimian primates first because these are the forms with which there is the greatest field experience and the best anatomical information at close to the species level. The method is, however, readily applicable to the Anthropoidea.

CHARLES E. OXNARD
Centre for Human Biology
The University of Western Australia
Nedlands, Australia

Acknowledgments

We are most grateful to M. D. Rose and A. C. Walker for their extended critical comments on the manuscript, and again to Walker for the loan of film material. F. P. Lisowski has been a major source of discussion and inspiration.

It is a pleasure to thank Marsha Greaves, Claire Vanderslice, and Joan Hives, who have provided depictions of some of the animals. Special thanks go to Erika Oller, who is responsible for most of the more recent drawings of prosimians. Among the many illustrations, her artistic style is easily recognized.

Eleanor M. Oxnard and Shirley Y. Tong Crompton have provided invaluable secretarial, editorial, and bibliographic assistance. Vanessa Hayes and Christine Runnion have been especially helpful in rooting out errors from the final manuscript.

The original fieldwork was supported by grants to Robin H. Crompton from the L. S. B. Leakey Fund, the Lee Foundation Fund, and the World Wildlife Fund. The overall research program has been supported for several years by two National Institutes of Health Biomedical Research Support Grants, and by University Professorship Funds and a Faculty Research and Innovation Fund Grant from the University of Southern California to Charles E. Oxnard. His most recent support stems from the Department of Anatomy and Human Biology and the Centre for Human Biology, The University of Western Australia, and from the Australian National Health and Medical Research Council and the Raine Foundation. Crompton's current programs are supported by the University of Liverpool Research Development Fund, the Nuffield Foundation, the Erna and Victor Hasselblad Foundation, the United Kingdom Medical Research Council, and the Science and Energy Research Council.

Oxnard thanks Lord Zuckerman, OM, KCB, MD, DSc, FRS, for his continuing interest over many years. Lord Zuckerman laid the foundation for quantitative biological studies of this type, and even now continues to support these new analytical studies of biological form and function.

Animal Lifestyles and Anatomies

1   The Interface between Lifestyles and Anatomies

The shape, dimensions, and form—the anatomies—of our bodies are in large part related to the activities—the lifestyles—that we undertake. These activities include the way we move, the way we feed, and the way we manipulate the external universe. Most of the characteristics of our anatomies that cannot be related to our current lifestyles are an inheritance from the different anatomies and lifestyles of our ancestors. We will investigate the interface between anatomies and lifestyles in the musculoskeletal system by identifying and utilizing three essential elements: (1) measurement and comparison of the anatomy of the musculoskeletal system itself, (2) measurement and comparison of the activities in which the musculoskeletal system participates, and finally (3) measurement and comparison of the specific parts of the external universe in which the activities occur.

The first of these elements is clearly the most straightforward, dealing as it does with tangible biological structures. They are discrete, at least at the level of the whole organism, and they are the purview of classical comparative anatomy and one of its modern descendants, comparative functional morphometrics.

The second element is more complex. It involves understanding the physical and biological responses of the musculoskeletal system to the external and internal forces engendered by animal activity. It includes the mechanical characteristics of the activities or "performances," and their patterns of frequency and distribution. We can readily identify in this second element such newer fields as biomechanics and kinesiology.

The third element, however, falls with behavioral ecology, rather than in the interface between biology and mechanics. It is exceedingly complex. The external universe within which the performances of the musculoskeletal system occur, includes both the relevant physical characteristics of the space or habitat, and the wider behavioral or adaptive roles that such performances play in the lifestyle of the animal.

It is hardly surprising that it is the first of these three elements that has received the greatest attention and which is the furthest developed. Dissection of cadavers and measurement of animal forms, though not necessarily easy in an absolute sense, seem easy in comparison with the other elements. The second element, involving biomechanical performance, is both technologically and inherently more complex. This is because biological materials are not uniform or simple in their mechanical characteristics, unlike the earlier materials on which most engineering science was based. And the third element, the behavioral and ecological, is notoriously time-consuming and inexact to study. These elements share with the experimentation of biophysics and biomechanics, the ethical and practical problems involved in the scarcity and extinction of subject materials, as the world's habitats steadily diminish. The problems of studying the anatomy of museum specimens are minimal in comparison. And yet it is axiomatic that all three elements must ultimately be involved in the study of the evolution and adaptation of organisms.

Certainly no one person can hope to apply each kind of approach on a large enough number of species to make global comparisons meaningful. It is almost certain that many primate species will pass close to, or even into, extinction before they can be adequately studied. We therefore present this book, both as a cooperative exploration of methodology which may stimulate further thinking about approaches to the study of the musculoskeletal system, and as a direct contribution to an understanding of primate organismal biology.

The book began in discussions between Oxnard and Crompton among the mists, crags, and rains of Lushan, one of the Sacred Mountains of China, while we were guests of the Chinese Anatomical Society at its 1982 congress. Talk continued in the dry heat of the garden of a Southern California hacienda in Pasadena, a year later. And further progress on the book ensued through more detailed discussions on quantitative methods in biology and on theoretical tropical ecology between Oxnard and Lieberman at the University of Southern California, Los Angeles.

Naturally enough, these discussions centered on the commonalities, limitations, and prospects of our own previous investigations. It is most appropriate, therefore, to lay out the reasons for our present approach in the same, semihistorical, form.

Locomotor Classifications

We have said that the classical approach, that of measurement and comparison of the musculoskeletal system itself, is methodologically and conceptually the least complex. It has certainly been carried on for the longest time and, in that sense, is the most advanced. But it has never, in practice, existed in isolation. For investigators have always known that it is meaningless to assemble, classify, and compare a set of observations of the form and dimensions of the locomotor system without reference to function (movement and posture).

Early workers such as Mollison (1910) were, of course, perfectly aware of this fact. Such comparative anatomists were confronted with collections of animals, some of which were evidently similar in gross morphology. Behavioral information was available about only the most striking or most well-known performances of a very few members of each group. More often than not, therefore, groupings of animals, based essentially upon morphology, were assigned names from visual impressions of the dominant locomotor pattern of relatively well-known members of the groups. Classifications of locomotor morphologies based upon such familiar terms as "springers," "climbers," and "leapers" were the result.

The implication of such a classification is that the significant commonalities of the morphologies of each group's members are formed by a dominant behavior which they all share, and by which the group is named. The German anatomists of the 1930s (e.g., Priemel 1937) were already aware that the mechanical consequences of the "typical" movement pattern were the means by which a typical group morphology might be molded. And this was reiterated by other workers such as Campbell (1937).

Simultaneously, the work of Carpenter (1934) and others was beginning to alert comparative anatomists to the rich diversity of behavior in the free-ranging primates. The traditional approach to musculoskeletal anatomy received a further major boost during the Second World War, in the elaboration of techniques that had been invented in the thirties (e.g., Fisher 1936; Mahalanobis 1936; Hotelling 1936), and eventually in the development of a technology termed multivariate statistical analysis. In part, this was a by-product of military anthropology and psychological testing.

This, then, was the background against which Oxnard, together with colleagues at Birmingham, England, began his studies of primate limb anatomy. Essentially traditional, classificatory approaches to morphological analysis were used not only to examine the general relationship between structure and function in living species (e.g., Ashton and Oxnard 1958, 1963) but also to help deduce likely locomotor behavior of fossil forms (e.g., Napier and Davis 1959).

Modifications of locomotor classifications

The traditional concept of the locomotor classification can still be used with profit to highlight apparent a priori associations between form and behavior. For example, Tables 1 and 2 taken together correlate a single gross behavioral characteristic with an individual relative limb dimension. This type of comparison, summarized by Napier and Napier in 1985, was the way that such studies were carried out at that time.

But it has become increasingly clear that the assumption of traditional classificatory approaches is overly simplistic. If used as a primary analytical tool, such classifications may obscure vitally important diversities and distinctions in behavior, function, and morphology. Thus, following the development of multivariate morphometric techniques, and with further information from functional anatomical studies, it transpired that categories established on the basis of the traditional method often contained species belonging to several distinct morphological complexes.

For example, the behavioral category "vertical clingers and leapers" (Na-

TABLE 1
An Early Classification of Primate Locomotion (after Napier and Napier
1967, 1985)

Category	Species (examples)	Activity
Vertical clinging and leaping	*Propithecus, Tarsius* and galagines	Vertical leaping in and between trees, ground hopping
Quadrupedalism (with subcategories)	lemurines, *Cebus* and *Cercopithecus*	Running and walking, climbing and springing
Brachiation (with subcategories)	*Hylobates, Pan, Pongo* and *Gorilla*	Frequent to occasional armswinging and arm climbing

TABLE 2
An Early Example of Relationships between Locomotor Classifications and
Anatomical Measures (after Napier and Napier 1967, 1985)

Locomotor Category	Specific Anatomical Measure (e.g., intermembral index)
Vertical clinging and leaping	55–65
Arboreal quadrupedalism	70–104
Brachiation	106–150

pier and Napier 1967) contained species belonging to, at that time, two (now three) distinct morphological groups (Oxnard 1973). The morphological characteristics of the animals in these newer groups implied that there existed several mechanically different types of saltatory specialization within the "vertical clinging and leaping" category. They also suggested that it would be unlikely that a single behavioral specialization, "vertical clinging and leaping," could describe each of the phenomena adequately (for overall review, see Oxnard 1983).

Difficulties such as these led Oxnard (Ashton and Oxnard 1964) to reject the use of the "overall" locomotor behavior of an animal as a classificatory criterion in favor of a more limited criterion: the function of individual anatomical regions. Ashton and Oxnard realized that, though two animals might engage in characteristic and frequent behavior similar enough to encourage their placement in a shared overall grouping such as "arboreal quadruped," consideration of regional anatomy might make it obvious, for example, that the function of the shoulder or the pelvis was distinct in each species. The overall behavioral classification obscures not only the existence of distinct morphologies, but also the probability of different functions in different anatomical regions. Thus, future field studies might not recognize

TABLE 3
An Example of a Regional Functional Locomotor Classification (after
Ashton and Oxnard 1964; see also Zuckerman et al. 1973, Oxnard 1983)

Locomotor Category	Species (examples)
Upper limb function, ability to hang by arms	*Pongo* and *Cacajao* together with *Hylobates* and *Ateles*
Lower limb function, ability to hang by legs	*Pongo* and *Cacajao* but not *Hylobates* and *Ateles*

different behavioral and adaptive roles of the shoulder or hip complexes in
each species if overall groups are used.

The classificatory use of function in a single anatomical region results, of
course, in the development of a new classification for each anatomical part
under study. A simple example is presented in Table 3. If we assume that
the functional category has to do with upper limbs, then orangutans (*Pongo*)
and uakaris (*Cacajao*) share features with gibbons (*Hylobates*) and spider
monkeys (*Ateles*). All these creatures commonly hang by their upper limbs.
They can be considered to be in an "upper-limb hanging group." But when
the functional category relates to lower limbs, orangutans and uakaris differ
from gibbons and spider monkeys. This is because, while the former pair
both frequently engage in hindlimb suspension, the latter only rarely do so.
The first two are in a "lower-limb hanging group," the second two are not.

Again, if we use the simpler method of examining individual anatomical
features that was generally current in the 1930s (and sometimes is used
even today), then it is easy to find individual characteristics that seem to
relate to such classifications. For example, if we study a single dimension,
relative hand length (as from the data of Napier and Napier 1967), we find
that the most arm-hanging species differ from the least arm-hanging forms
in this measure (see Table 4). We also find, in the same way, that the most
leg-hanging species differ from the least leg-hanging species in relative foot
length. In summary then, though gibbons and spider monkeys fall with the
orangutan and uakari in a morphological feature (hand length) and in a
functional feature (arm-hanging), they fall into the opposite group when
foot length and leg-hanging are considered. The picture becomes somewhat
muddied if we start to include creatures that do something else with their
hindlimbs, for instance, leaping. Nevertheless, the regional anatomical approach was soon seen to be a fruitful one for the study of the association
between anatomies and behaviors.

It might seem, however, that this idea could generate as many classifications as we had questions. If that were so, then such categorization could
be taken further and further into more detailed levels. It might end up as

TABLE 4

Examples of Relationships between Regional Locomotor Classifications
and Regional Anatomical Measures (after Oxnard 1983)

Regional Functional Group	Species	Anatomical Measure
		Relative hand length
More arm-hanging: acrobats	*Pongo*	53
	Cacajao	40
	Hylobates	59
	Ateles	48
More arm-hanging: all acrobats		40–59
Less arm-hanging: quadrupeds		28–32
		Relative foot length
Leg-hanging	*Pongo*	61
	Cacajao	60
No leg-hanging	*Hylobates*	50
	Ateles	48
Leg-hanging: some acrobats		60–61
No leg-hanging: other acrobats		48–50
No leg-hanging: quadrupeds		42–50

an artificial and cumbersome exercise. In fact, of course, there are limits to the degree to which the classifications can or ought to be broken down. For instance, though one might think that the functional units of animal locomotion were such that forelimb groupings might be further divided into shoulder, arm, and forearm groupings separately, in fact, these three regions are all markedly similar to one another. They are all part of the functional unit comprising the set of levers of the upper limb. It is only when we come to the function of the hand that a new regional division is important.

In the same way, though we might expect the different anatomies of the hip, thigh, and leg, for example, to generate a series of different classifications, in fact they do not. The functional unit is the set of levers of the lower limb, and each of the subunits provides that picture. The more complex function of the foot, like the hand, should be considered separately.

These ideas notwithstanding, however, further study made it clear that what we are dealing with here are not discrete behavioral classes to which an animal either does or does not belong, but continuous functional spectra within given anatomical regions (Oxnard 1975). This nonclassificatory approach to the comparison of locomotor behavior allows a far more flexible description of the character of a given species with respect to any behavioral trait. Thus, as the morphometric studies of Oxnard developed, this idea of the functional spectrum proved a most valuable way of describing and comparing the behavioral side of the behavioral-anatomical interface (summarized in Oxnard 1983).

The visual immediacy of the functional spectrum is particularly useful. For example, figure 1.1 shows the arm and leg behavioral tendencies modeled as, respectively, a band-shaped spectrum and a star-shaped spectrum. The similarity of these behavioral patterns to morphological patterns derived from multivariate analysis of measurements of arm and leg (fig. 1.2) is striking.

A particular utility of this approach is surely in the prediction of behavior when only morphological data are known, or vice versa. One especially important usage of the multivariate method is the distinguishing of unique combinations of character-states (witness, in fig. 1.3, the isolated position of the functionally and structurally unique genus *Homo* when each of the plots in fig. 1.2 are viewed from another vantage point).

Further inadequacies of classificatory and other univariate approaches became apparent as the diversity that exists below the generic level was revealed. Thus, Oxnard (1967) recognized that differences in degrees of arboreality, of frequencies of acrobatic or leaping activity, etc. could be discerned among the species of genera such as *Cercopithecus, Presbytis, Cercocebus,* and *Macaca.* These were all, at that time, combined by most workers in the single group "generalized arboreal quadrupeds."

Oxnard showed that there was considerable association between these behavioral differences and the differences in anatomical variables within each of these genera. For example, Table 5 shows how a single variable, scapular width, varies with degree of arboreality in a series of more and less arboreal Old World monkeys. Such an association was not anywhere as

TABLE 5
Relationships between Quadrupedal Differences and Anatomical Measures (after Oxnard 1967)

Category	Anatomical Measure (e.g., mediolateral width of scapula
Least arboreal *Cercopithecus* species	6.1
Most arboreal *Cercopithecus* species	5.4
Least arboreal *Cercocebus* species	6.7
Most arboreal *Cercocebus* species	5.6
Least arboreal *Macaca* species	6.4
Most arboreal *Macaca* species	5.1

Note: Narrower scapula in more arboreal species

Fig. 1.1. Models of locomotor function in primate upper and lower limbs, respectively. Primate upper limbs seem to function along a simple bandlike spectrum from more compression, less arm-raising, and lower quadrant mobility (as in baboons and tarsiers), to less compression (more tension), more arm-raising and higher quadrant mobility (as in gibbons and orangutans). Similarly, primate lower limbs function in a starlike spectrum as indicated.

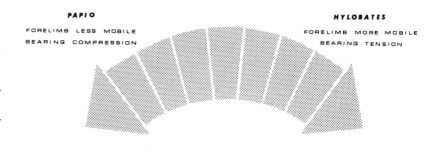

clear as when many variables were studied together, but it nevertheless could be seen to exist.

Similar correlated distinctions in behavior and morphology were revealed in several genera of monkeys by Manaster (1976), and in many prosimian genera by Oxnard et al. (1981a and b), who examined many variables and many species together. And they were also shown, although to lesser degree, by Fleagle (1976, 1979), Rodman (1979), and Mittermeier (1978) in ex-

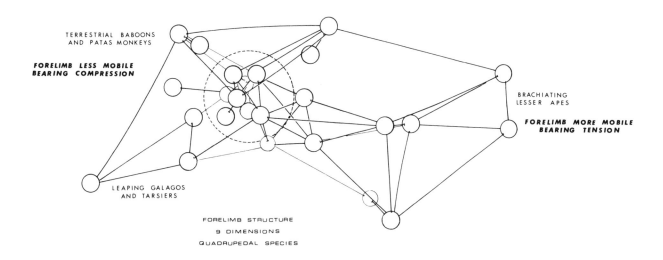

TERRESTRIAL BABOONS
AND PATAS MONKEYS

***FORELIMB LESS MOBILE
BEARING COMPRESSION***

BRACHIATING
LESSER APES

***FORELIMB MORE MOBILE
BEARING TENSION***

LEAPING GALAGOS
AND TARSIERS

FORELIMB STRUCTURE

9 DIMENSIONS

QUADRUPEDAL SPECIES

Fig. 1.2. Studies of locomotor anatomy in primate upper and lower limbs, respectively. Primate upper limbs, as seen from morphometric analysis of upper limb proportions, arrange the species in a band similar to the functional model in figure 1.1. Likewise, morphometric analysis of primate lower limbs arranges the species as a star similar to the functional model in figure 1.1.

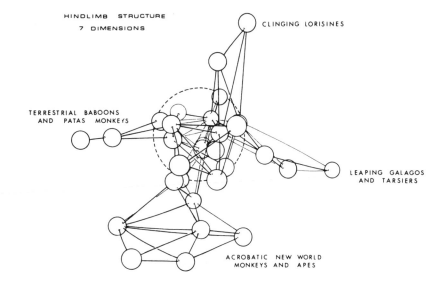

HINDLIMB STRUCTURE
7 DIMENSIONS

CLINGING LORISINES

TERRESTRIAL BABOONS
AND PATAS MONKEYS

LEAPING GALAGOS
AND TARSIERS

ACROBATIC NEW WORLD
MONKEYS AND APES

amining pairs of species and individual anatomical characteristics one by one. Such associations, when examined in many groups and using many variables, were shown even to extend to different populations of a single subspecies (Albrecht 1980).

A final example of the degree of complexity that exists within groups of animals previously established as a single locomotor category—generalized quadrupedalism—can be seen in Table 6 and figures 1.4 and 1.5. Table 6

TABLE 6
Locomotor Variations within Quadrupeds (after Oxnard 1975)

Category	Species (examples)
Old World Monkeys	
A. Least arboreal	*Cercopithecus aethiops, Macaca mulatta, Presbytis entellus*
B. Intermediately arboreal	*Cercopithecus mitis*
C. Most arboreal	*Cercopithecus diana, Presbytis cristatus*
*New World Monkeys**	
A. Least acrobatic	*Callithrix, Leontocebus*
B. Intermediately acrobatic	*Pithecia, Cacajao*
C. Most acrobatic	*Cebus, Allouatta*

*Excepting the atelines (spider and woolly spider monkeys), which are more correctly described as New World brachiating species

provides the subcategories (or spectrum) within generalized quadrupedalism for each group of monkeys. Figures 1.4 and 1.5 show how these subcategories are reflected in studies examining the several species and several anatomical characteristics taken together.

In each of the series of Old and New World monkeys that were previously classed as "generalized arboreal quadrupeds," the behavioral subcategories labelled A, B, and C as defined in Table 6, are linearly associated in studies of both the forelimb (fig. 1.4) and the hindlimb (fig. 1.5). The distinctions here are much clearer than in the univariate studies, presumably exactly because more information is summated by the morphometric method.

In addition, in both forelimbs and hindlimbs, the relationships between the morphologies of groups A, B, C are seen to be quite different in Old and New World monkeys. This suggests that the patterns of adaptation are different in each. The pattern in the New World monkeys resembles, in smaller degree, that existing among the primates as a whole. The pattern in the Old World monkeys is unique unto itself, implying that something special occurred within the evolution of this group that is not replicated throughout the Order. It is possible this may have included two or more cyclical changes between terrestrial and arboreal adaptations over millions of years (Oxnard 1983).

So far we have dealt with the first element in studies of the primate musculoskeletal system: measurement and comparison of the musculoskeletal system itself. We have seen that in order to interpret the patterns of morphology that exist, morphometrists have been forced to utilize behavioral categories. They have been forced, in other words, to adopt information from the second element: measurement and comparison of the activities in which the musculoskeletal system takes part. They have had to do this in a

Fig. 1.3. The uniqueness of humans, clearly evident from consideration of a free upper limb and bipedal lower limb, is also evident as an anatomical outlier when the band and the star of figure 1.2 are viewed from other vantage points.

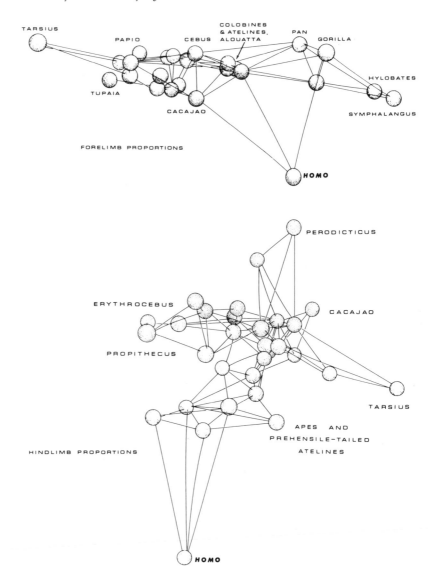

very non-quantitative and almost anecdotal manner. Yet they have been able to progress from the artificial idea of the group to the somewhat less artificial concept of the spectrum.

The retreat from locomotor classifications

This failure of the classificatory approach to express clearly enough the adaptive complexity and functional diversity of the primate locomotor system, led to a reaction against locomotor classifications. Several workers felt that in order to study adaptation of the locomotor system, the whole locomotor repertoire of a species and its behavioral and adaptive milieu should

Fig. 1.4. Morphometric analyses of the proportions of primate upper limbs, when demonstrated through the medium of the high-dimensional display (for full descriptions see Andrews 1972, 1973, and Oxnard, 1975, 1983), show consistent arrangements of the different New and Old World monkeys as defined in Table 6. With this method of display, each species is defined by a curved plot. Similarity among species can be seen by the narrowness of the envelope (shaded area) that encloses their similar plots. When species are different this can be seen by the broad envelopes indicating wide separations between their very different plots. Intermediate species or groups of species can be seen by plots or envelopes that are intermediate. The degree of similarity or difference of two plots at any vertical point on the graph is shown by the standard deviation unit marker. The area between the plots is the generalized distance between the species.

The upper graph shows the shaded envelopes for the plots of (A) least arboreal, (B) intermediately arboreal, and (C) most arboreal Old World monkeys, and (A) least acrobatic, (B) intermediately acrobatic, and (C) most acrobatic New World monkeys. *Cebus*, the capuchin, is not easily characterized. Its individual plot has been graphed, and it seems to fall between groups B and C of the New World monkeys, which fits with what is known both structurally and functionally about this species. Though the overall relationships are linear from A to C in each group of monkeys, they are differently arranged between each.

The high-dimensional display is a way of recognizing similarities in results that have a dimensionality greater than three, and for which, therefore, three dimensional models cannot be constructed. Each type of animal is shown as a curved plot. The shaded envelopes contain all the curved plots for each of the alphabetically labeled groups of animals.

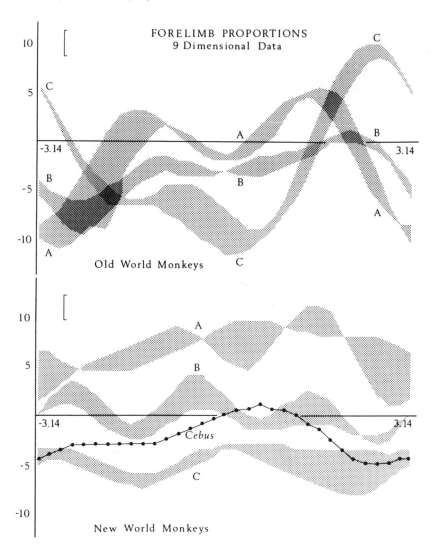

be systematically recorded. Locomotor behavior was thus recognized as a field of study in its own right, not just as an aid to locomotor classification and as an adjunct to morphometrics.

Thus the third element in studies of the musculoskeletal system was initiated: the description of the behavioral and environmental milieu within which locomotor performance occurs. With the growth of field studies of primates, it had long been apparent to investigators such as Ripley (1967) that locomotion and posture could not be readily divorced from other behaviors such as play, feeding, and social interaction. For Ripley, leaping behavior was, indeed, to be seen within the context of locomotion and posture narrowly defined. But it was also appreciated as an element of foraging behavior, and in relation to ecological factors such as food dispersal. And Napier and Napier (1967) pointed out that the structural characteristics of

Fig. 1.5. This figure shows similar information for lower limbs and with all the same explanations and conventions as in figure 1.4.

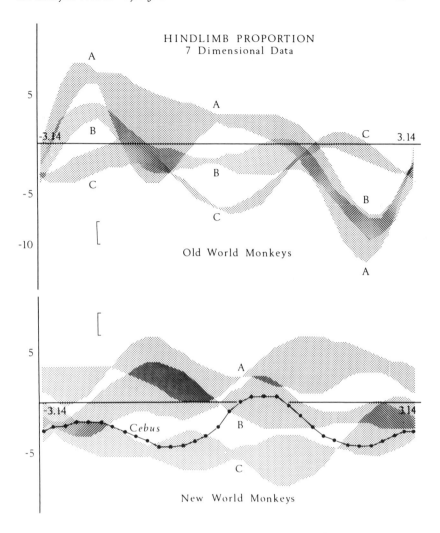

the forest stratum in which the animal lives, in particular, its continuity or discontinuity, are directly relevant to an understanding of primate locomotion.

It therefore became common for fieldworkers not primarily interested in anatomical locomotor studies to gather data on patterns of movement and support use (e.g., Bearder 1974; Kinzey 1976; Charles-Dominique 1977). But soon comparative anatomists themselves began to go into the field to analyze at first hand structural-functional relationships in the locomotor system. Fleagle (1976, 1979) worked on relationships among support utilization, locomotion, and locomotor anatomy in *Presbytis* and *Pithecia*. Morbeck did similar work on *Colobus* (1979), and Niemitz (1979 et seq.) on *Tarsius bancanus*.

A means of summarizing the locomotor behavior of a species was still needed. Prost (1967) had attempted to set out a methodology for such summaries. He specifically contrasted "critical locomotor habits" with "frequent locomotor habits." Rose (1973) analyzed the different patterns of locomotor behavior that could be subsumed under the category "quadruped." And, finally, Walker (1974, 1979) provided verbal summaries of the locomotion of numerous prosimians from field and film observations. Walker, in particular, aimed at replicable and objective summaries of locomotor behavior in its broad sense, and in 1979 he provided a quantitative summary and statistical analysis of locomotor patterns and support use in *Galago demidovii*.

It was as Walker's doctoral student that Crompton began a field study of locomotor behavior in two species of *Galago* in the Northern Transvaal of Southern Africa. Initially, the project was intended simply to gather quantitative data on locomotor behavior similar to what Fleagle (1976) had garnered for *Presbytis*. Crompton hoped to go further, however, in relating any quantitative differences in the frequency of movement patterns, support use, stratum of the forest, and other features found to exist between the two congeners, to differences in the musculoskeletal anatomy, such as muscle insertions and moments about joint centers.

It soon became evident, however, that distinctions in locomotor behavior between the two species were demonstrably linked to the foraging strategy appropriate to each in a strongly seasonal environment. It also became clear that relationships between body size, energetics, and dietary quality had to be included. And dispersion of food resources and the structural characteristics of the arboreal zones in which the food resources were distributed were seen as yet further important. Thus, locomotor adaptation, in its broadest sense, became an ecological problem.

This approach (Crompton 1984) was echoed in other studies, notably by Garber (1984) in work published in the same volume (Rodman and Cant 1984) dealing with adaptations for foraging in nonhuman primates. Crompton's study also demonstrated for the first time that quantitative differences in locomotion and habitat utilization existed between conspecific animals of different age groups (Crompton 1983). These were possibly related to body size differences (a possibility originally suggested by Ripley 1967). But it is also possible that they were related to behavioral development (noted by Oxnard 1973).

In this type of detailed and broad field study, comparing each member of a pair of closely related species is undoubtedly a good tool for the close analysis of the process of behavioral-anatomical evolution. It has, however, distinct limitations. It is always possible to locate distinctions in morphology and behavior when two species are compared. But such differences are not necessarily causally related. Though this type of study undoubtedly usually works out an accurate picture of locomotor adaptation in species pairs, as has been discussed by Oxnard (1983), further testing by multiple comparisons is essential. Only such wider investigations can show if the hypotheses and generalizations derived from such pair-wise comparisons are significant and generally valid.

An Alternative Strategy

Let us review the situation as the three of us saw it as a result of our extended and collaborative discussions.

The morphometric element was well advanced, and multivariate statistical methods offered an efficient way of handling multiple species comparisons and complex combinations of variables. The techniques appeared particularly powerful in distinguishing shared patterns of morphology, and in highlighting unique character-state combinations. However, such analyses were meaningless unless morphological comparisons could be functionally interpreted on the basis of a comparable set of data about locomotor activity.

Broadly defined, locomotor activity, the second element, included kinesiological and other biomechanical approaches to the analysis of the form of primate locomotor performance. These approaches are technologically complex. Though we believe that they are an essential part of our own future research (and this research is being carried out by Crompton and his students), we agreed that they were not yet well enough advanced to be systematically employed at this time in studying the major morphological patterns revealed by morphometric analysis.

Quite extensive data, both quantitative and qualitative, were available about the third element—the environmental and ecological context. These data included information about the pattern and frequency of primate locomotor performances. They also included the behavioral and structural context of these performances. And they included the diet that the performances used in garnering from the environment. Taken together, these data encompassed a good deal of the third element. But there existed no satisfactory approach to their summary and analysis in a form that allowed reasonably direct comparison with morphology.

As we have observed, simple, univariate descriptors of striking or "typical" behaviors of well-known species had at first appeared sufficient to order grossly similar morphologies into locomotor categories. But it was soon apparent that the musculoskeletal morphology of the whole animal is not associated solely with one or two dominant "overall" behaviors. Rather, the musculoskeletal system should be considered as a series of regional functional complexes. Each has distinct roles to play in the diverse locomotor performances by which an organism interacts with its environment.

Further, increased sophistication in morphometric analysis had revealed a growing diversity of morphological patterns within gross locomotor categories. This suggested that the morphologies did not reflect any single biomechanical pattern or behavioral phenomenon. And correlated patterns of morphological and behavioral distinctions had been discerned at ever-finer taxonomic levels.

It was finally apparent that locomotor behavior could not simply be examined at the level of isolated performances, but must be studied in the context of other behaviors in which locomotion had a role. This included feeding behavior and diet. And it included the structure of the habitat within which locomotion occurs. Neither traditional nor modified locomotor classificatory approaches, nor the functional spectrum, could efficiently summarize anything like an adequate amount of this type of multidimensional data. And though detailed studies of individual species or species groups could provide efficient quantitative summaries of behavior, such verbally based (even if quantified) summaries as those provided in Walker's (1979) and Crompton's (1983, 1984) studies would rapidly become unmanageable when large numbers of species were involved.

It was thus essential that extensive comparative analyses of locomotor behavior be performed if significant results were to be obtained. But we could not afford to wait until standardized, quantified summaries, such as the latter, were available for the great majority of primate species. The sad truth is that they will not now be collected before the extinction of many species in their natural habitat.

Knowing that it is difficult to characterize anatomy adequately using only a single or few descriptors, but knowing also that anatomy can be adequately described when a multidimensional multivariate approach is employed, we thought it reasonable to attempt to describe the available data on locomotor behavior, habitat utilization, and diet in the same way. In this book, therefore, we present a method to describe the locomotor activities of animals using many variables, rather than the single descriptors of simple classifications. And we present multivariable and multivariate ways of analyzing them to produce the succinct data reduction and elimination of redundancy that have already resulted in the morphometric investigations.

The development of such a procedure for lifestyle information then allows associations to be drawn between lifestyles and anatomies when similar and full multidimensional descriptions are available for each. Of course, the relationship between multidimensional representations of lifestyles and multidimensional representations of anatomies is unlikely to be direct or simple. But their comparison may be easier and more accurate than when anatomies or lifestyles are compared using only one or two dimensions on each side.

2 Activity, Habitat Utilization, and Dietary Preference in Prosimians

Fig. 2.1. An instance of vertical clinging.

The same sequence of investigations that we have described in the first chapter for the primates as a whole, also characterizes prosimians specifically. The earliest attempts to understand prosimian locomotion revolved around global concepts such as "vertical clinger and leaper" (Napier and Napier 1967; Table 7), which included a number of prosimians: tarsiers, bushbabies, and indriids. The descriptor was useful for understanding broad structural adaptations (e.g., Napier and Walker 1967). (See figures 2.1, 2.2, and 2.3.)

More recently, however, this category has been shown to hide important differences (as suggested first by Oxnard 1973, and Stern and Oxnard 1973; and later by Oxnard, German, Jouffroy, and Lessertisseur 1981, and Oxnard, German, and McArdle 1981). These studies on prosimian locomotor anatomy used the notions of the regional and functional grouping and the functional spectrum. They led to the recognition that several different kinds of anatomy, and hence, perhaps, several different kinds of functional adaptation, exist within the category "vertical clinger and leaper."

Tarsiers and bushbabies, indriids and sportive lemurs, and cheirogaleines can all be identified behaviorally as vertical clinging and leaping animals. But they cling and leap in different ways with different ecological consequences (fig. 2.4). This is most easily seen through inspection of the flight phase during long leaps. Such postures have been frequently captured on film. Tarsiers and some bushbabies use curled-up positions during flight. Indriids employ stretched-out positions in the flight phase. Cheirogaleines in mid-flight have the limbs hanging down "quadrupedally." Though it is generally more difficult to document them in the field, other aspects of leaping that are biomechanically more important, for instance, takeoff and landing, are likely also to differ. And there are certainly a series of other loco-

Fig. 2.2. Leaping posture.

TABLE 7
Primate Locomotor Classification (after Napier and Napier)

Locomotor Category	Activity	Genera
Vertical clinging and leaping	Leaping in trees and hopping on the ground	*Avahi, Galago, Hapalemur, Lepilemur, Propithecus, Indri, Tarsius*
Quadrupedalism	Moving on four limbs; many subcategories	Most remaining prosimians, most monkeys

Fig. 2.3. Several examples of vertical
clinging and leaping.

motor and postural differences not directly a part of leaping at all, but that differentiate these various leaping species (for review see Oxnard 1983).

The result of all this is that it is possible to subdivide "vertical clinging and leaping" into three modes (Table 8). Yet even here, data are problematical. For example, it was not initially clear to Oxnard and colleagues with which group the genus *Hapalemur* was most closely associated, and it was therefore included in two possible positions. As information improved, one species, *Lepilemur,* was moved, in 1973, from being a member of a quadrupedal group (Oxnard and colleagues) to a leaping group (Oxnard).

These studies also show that these different species employ, appropriately, different anatomies for the different versions of vertical clinging and leaping. Morphometrically they are divided into the same three groups: (1) tarsiers and bushbabies, (2) indriids, (3) cheirogaleines. Each is arranged around a central group of more quadrupedal lemurs (reviewed in Oxnard 1983; fig. 2.5).

It is our view that there are likely to be yet further differences among these leaping species. The additional differences may rest in the other things that they do. Thus, vertical clinging and leaping may be differentiated not only because vertical clinging and leaping is a biomechanically

TABLE 8

Locomotor Trends in Prosimian Leaping after Oxnard (Oxnard, German, and McArdle 1981; Oxnard, German, Jouffroy, and Lessertisseur 1981)

Trend of indriid-type leaping from maximum (left) to minimum (right)
(Large upward leaps, stretched-out body posture during leaps)

Avahi	*Lepilemur*	*Lemur variegatus*
Propithecus	*Lemur catta*	
Indri		

Trend of galagine-type leaping from maximum (left) to minimum (right)
(Large upward leaps, curled-up body posture during leaps)

Galago senegalensis	*Galago demidovii*	*Galago crassicaudatus*
G. elegantulus		*?Hapalemur?*
Tarsius		

Trend of cheirogaleine-type leaping from maximum (left) to minimum (right)
(Leaps mostly downward, limbs hanging down, often begin and end in running)

Microcebus	*Cheirogaleus medius*	*Cheirogaleus major*
		?Hapalemur?

Note: Positions ascribed to genera are only approximate; there is no comparability in degrees of leaping between the major groups.

Note: *?Hapalemur?* has two possible positions.

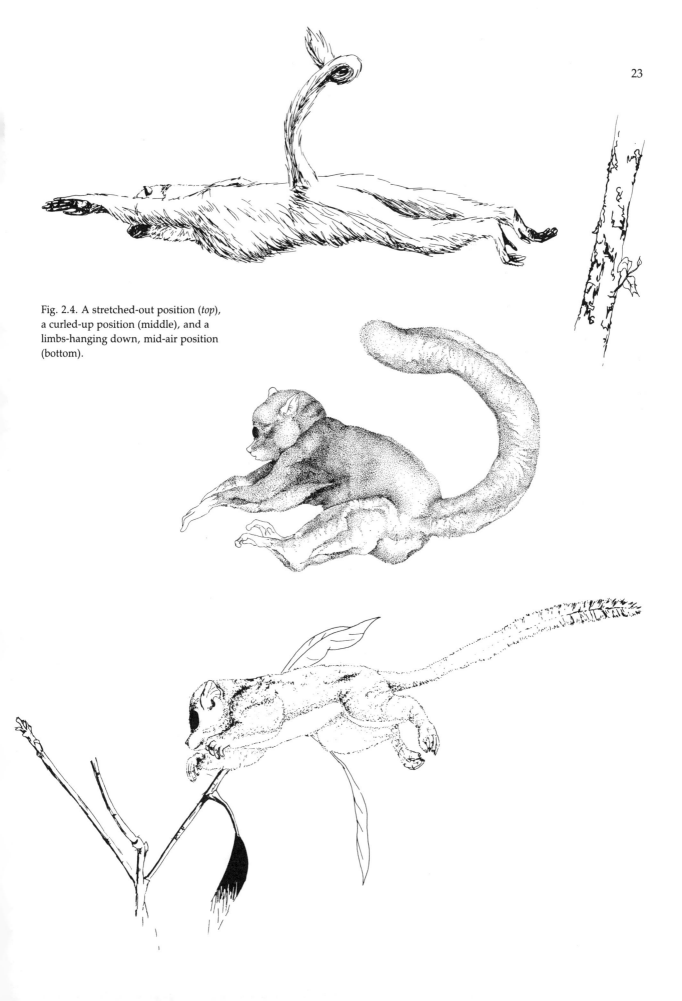

Fig. 2.4. A stretched-out position (*top*), a curled-up position (middle), and a limbs-hanging down, mid-air position (bottom).

Fig. 2.5. An anatomical (morphometric) analysis of overall limb proportions shows three more-leaping groups: indriids, cheirogaleines, and galagines-plus-tarsiers, arranged in a star-like fashion around a single centrally located less-leaping group of lemurs.

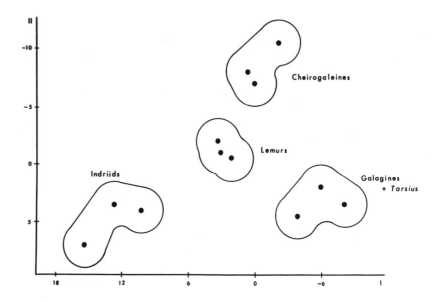

The axes of this plot are the first two canonical variates scaled in standard deviation units. The group of indriids comprise the genera *Propithecus, Avahi,* and *Indri.* The cheirogaleines consist of the genus *Microcebus,* and the species *Cheirogaleus medius* and *major.* The galagines plus tarsiers include the genera *Tarsius, Galago,* and *Euoticus* (in this study, *Galago elegantulus*). The group of lemurs include the genera *Lemur, Hapalemur,* and *Lepilemur.* More detailed study of this result (see Oxnard, German, Jouffroy, and Lessertisseur 1981) placed these last two genera as lying toward some of the more-leaping groups.

different activity in different species, but also because it is linked, in the various forms, with other quite different aspects of locomotion.

For example, one form of vertical clinging might be associated with one set of non-leaping activities, habitat choices, and dietary preferences. Another form might be associated with other non-leaping activities, habitats, and diets. In order to discover if such non-leaping factors also differentiate types of vertical clinging and leaping, we need "behavioral" descriptors that take account not only of leaping locomotion and its correlates, but also of many other features of locomotion, environment, and diet.

In this study we are attempting to go in the new direction just outlined by defining a new set of descriptors relating to the behavioral side of the behavioral-anatomical equation. A first set of parameters attempts to describe additional aspects of locomotor activities. A second set focuses on the characteristics of the habitat within which such activities occur. And a third set of parameters outlines the actual diet which the activities help the animal to procure from the habitat.

We have to be careful to distinguish between the animals' fundamental niche and their realized niche. For many species there are significant differences between these two. With respect to diet, there are species that are capable of eating, and actually may prefer, food sources that they do not use in their natural habitat due to competition. In this case, then, we must be careful to distinguish between dietary preferences and diet itself. And such a caveat applies to all the other features that we have examined.

The Raw Data

To obtain this information on locomotion, behavior, and diet, we have first extracted from the literature, in a standardized manner, the available data for each species on each kind of parameter. There are undoubtedly a number of different ways in which individual components of locomotor activities, the environmental arena within which they are carried out, and the dietary components at which they are aimed, can be categorized. Our particular choice of parameters, however, has been governed by the quality of the information available, and by our concentration on those elements we believe likely to have functional (biomechanical) implications for the anatomies of the specific animals themselves.

We recognize that the list of parameters will have to be modified as our understanding grows. We welcome the opportunity to expand our data as more information becomes available, and we encourage further research in that direction.

We also recognize some important limitations of this approach. First, the method currently places most emphasis on frequent activities, at the expense of those which may be infrequent. Yet infrequent activities may be critical in terms of maximum imposed loading of anatomical structures, or in terms of their significance for foraging or escaping, or other adaptively essential behaviors.

An example of such an infrequent activity is the "cantilevering" movement or "flag posture" (Martin 1972; Walker 1979; Crompton 1983) of some galagines and cheirogaleines. This posture is likely to produce very high bending moments on the leg and foot, and appears to be highly correlated with insect-feeding behavior in some bushbabies (Crompton 1983). But information about this activity is absent for most species. We feel that while some method of weighting poorly known variables is required, at present this is likely to introduce a subjective element into our analysis. Eventually there may be better data for features such as these, and we will be able to introduce them into future analyses. This type of problem is also amenable to laboratory investigation, although that might be a difficult task.

Second, our approach does not address directly the question of involvement of a "locomotor" structure or a "locomotor" performance in completely non-locomotor activities. This we have attempted to remedy by providing a discussion of such possible interrelationships individually for each species.

Again, however, we can see no way at the present time that this second problem can be treated on other than an individual species basis. Its solution depends on a more extensive knowledge than is currently available for most of our subject species.

These two problems notwithstanding, our method is straightforward and proceeds as follows. In each case, reviewing the literature for each species and each variable allows us to assess the degree to which each parameter is manifest (frequency of observation or occurrence) on a continuous scale from 0 to 10. When percent frequencies were available in the literature, these were used directly. When they were not available (as was usually the case), the qualitative descriptions were evaluated on the following basis. Most descriptions employ a very limited set of adjectives and adverbs, and these were given scores on the 0 to 10 scale so that, for example, "never" scored 0, "rarely" scored 1, "mostly" 5, and so on (see Table 9).

Certainly, the verbal *descriptions* that underlie these measures are heavily observer-dependent, but no alternative presents itself. We especially recognize that some error is introduced in using verbal descriptions that were translated from the author's own language. We have to assume some degree of repeatability in the way fieldworkers describe a phenomenon, otherwise there would be no value in such fieldwork. To a lesser extent the *scoring* is also observer-dependent, but we feel that several competent observers would not be likely to disturb overly much the rank order of a species based on the present literature.

In testing these best-estimate scores, we first relied on the similarity of our estimates resulting from familiarity with the literature as compared with personal experience in quantifying such parameters in field studies. And we secondly examined film and video records (our own as well as those of others) as a further check.

There is a special problem in scoring which relates to the zero category. Sometimes "0" or "never" really means "hardly ever" or "possibly occurs but never observed" *as far as the observer can tell*. Sometimes, however, "0" means not only "never observed" but also "cannot occur" or "truly never occurs" *as far as the observer can tell*. This is the difference between a zero that is the lower end of a quantitative spectrum and a zero that is qualitatively different from some apparently related quantitative spectrum. For example, though many prosimians leap, some leap infrequently enough, or leaps have not been observed for them, that they might be categorized as zero leapers. But the situation in a specific form such as *Perodicticus*, which not only does not leap but cannot leap (although it can "fall" from a branch), might also be scored as zero but is completely different. We have taken account of this difference in zero in our analyses.

The scoring part of the operation was performed by Crompton alone. This is likely to have had a significant moderating effect on error levels. Crompton (the only one experienced in primate fieldwork) also viewed the video and film records and used firsthand field experience for many of the subject species. Obviously, this exercise would be more accurate if performed exclusively on quantitative data and for all species in the field situation. This is, of course, a scarcely possible attainment.

TABLE 9
Scale for Scoring

Never	0.0
Rarely	0.1–0.2
Sometimes	0.5
Quite often	1.0
Commonly	2.0
Mostly	4.0–5.0
Dominated by	6.0
Almost exclusively	8.0
Exclusively	10.0

Summarizing Large Numbers of Parameters

It rapidly proves most difficult to visualize large numbers of parameters for each species using the standard verbal descriptors. We have, therefore, summarized the raw data, not by employing some overall average (as is inherent in the idea of a locomotor classification), but by grouping the information multidimensionally in a way that allows its entire complexity to be on view. At the same time this multidimensional method gives multivariable profiles that allow comparisons of individual species with one another.

These multidimensional first-order, "raw," visualizations are produced by graphing the different parameters as individual radii of polar coordinate plots. They result in "star-shaped envelopes" for each animal species. The particular form of the "star" or "envelope" for each species represents the totality of the activity, habitat, and dietary descriptors involved in its formation. One example is shown in figure 2.6, which also provides a key for the positions of each individual variable. (See Table 10 for variables.) This form is kept constant in every plot.

Fig. 2.6. Polar coordinate plot of raw data for a single species: *Galago senegalensis.*

The degree of a variable is shown along each radius. The variables are arranged (from three o'clock and in an anticlockwise direction) as leaping, forest stratum, supports, quadrupedalism, and diet. The variables are numbered from 1 to 17, as in Table 10. The eighteenth variable in Table 10, body weight, is not included in these plots, though it is used in certain analyses. The actual value of a variable is given by the number from 0 to 10 alongside the variable number, as determined in Table 9.

The principal information provided by these niche variables is given by the form of the envelope for the species; in the example in this figure it is shaped like a stalked leaf.

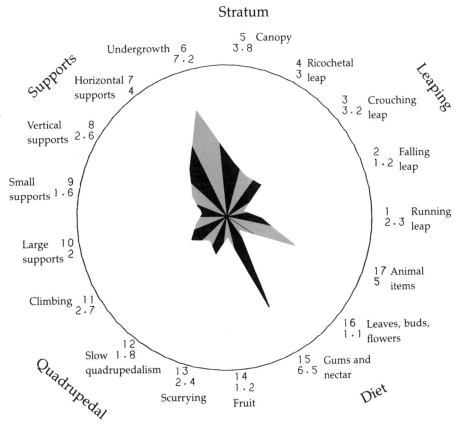

Fig. 2.7. Two species that are completely different show completely different envelopes.

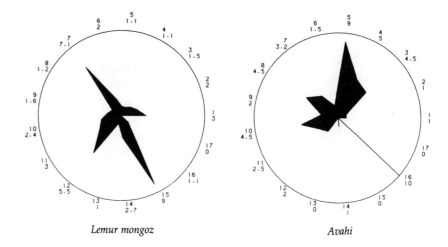

Lemur mongoz   *Avahi*

Fig. 2.8. Three species that form a tight group show very similar envelopes.

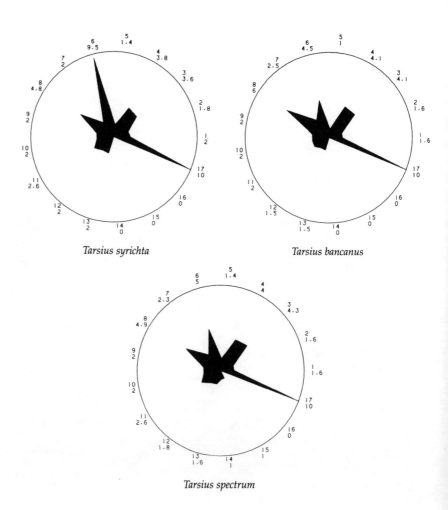

Tarsius syrichta   *Tarsius bancanus*

Tarsius spectrum

Notwithstanding its apparent complexity, such an envelope can be readily assimilated by eye. Comparison of two envelopes is relatively easy and allows comparison of one species with another. Thus, figure 2.7 shows two plots that are completely different from one another.

A group of basically similar envelopes are also easily picked out. They readily identify a group of species that are markedly similar to one another in most of the variables (fig. 2.8). Recognition of a sequence of gradually differing envelopes allows a spectrum of activity, habitat, and diet to be encompassed. An example of such a sequence is shown in figure 2.9. It can be recognized even though the different variables are changing in different ways as one passes along the sequence.

Fig. 2.9. Three species forming a linear array have envelopes that differ appropriately.

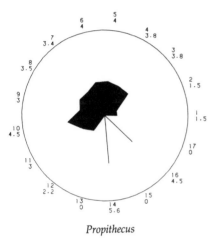

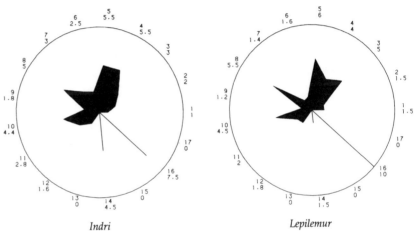

Propithecus   *Indri*   *Lepilemur*

TABLE 10
Variables

1. Running leap
2. Falling leap
3. Crouching leap
4. Ricochetal leap
5. Canopy
6. Undergrowth
7. Horizontal supports
8. Vertical supports
9. Small supports
10. Large supports
11. Climbing
12. Slow quadrupedalism
13. Scurrying
14. Fruit
15. Gums and nectar
16. Leaves, buds, flowers
17. Animal items
18. Body weight

Recognition of envelopes that differ slightly from their near neighbors but greatly from more distant ones allows recognition of a circular or doughnut-shaped arrangement. This is shown in figure 2.10, where there are smaller differences around the ring-shaped group, but large differences across it diametrically.

Discovery of individual envelopes that are totally different from all others presents information about species that are unique (e.g., fig. 2.11). In essence, broad overall similarities, intermediacies, and detailed coherent differences are easily assimilated through such diagrams.

This way of looking in a more detailed manner into the activities, habitats, and diets of the animals has parallels with the earlier attempt to understand locomotion using the regional locomotor spectrum. The regional locomotor spectrum allows us to see more detailed complexities inside overall locomotion by presenting the different "dimensions" of the anatomy involved in activities of the animals. These new profiles also allow us to see more detailed complexity inside overall locomotion by studying the different dimensions of the niche occupied by the animals.

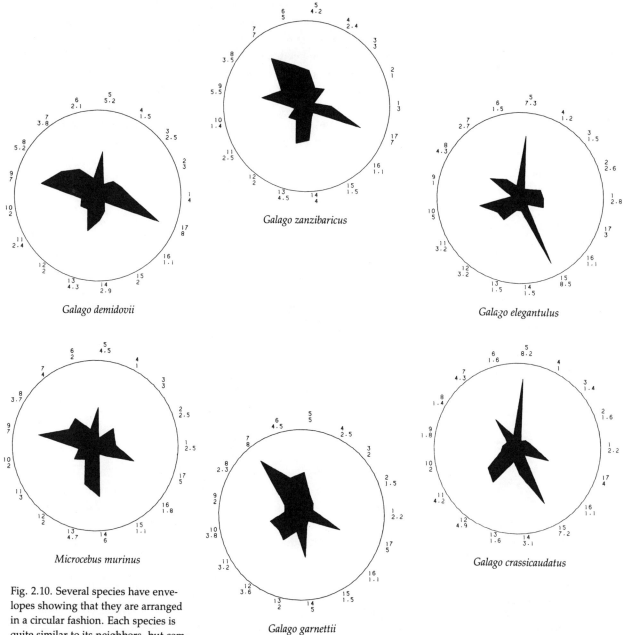

Galago zanzibaricus

Galago demidovii

Galago elegantulus

Microcebus murinus

Galago garnettii

Galago crassicaudatus

Fig. 2.10. Several species have envelopes showing that they are arranged in a circular fashion. Each species is quite similar to its neighbors, but completely different from its opposites.

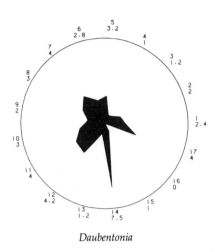

Daubentonia

Fig. 2.11. One species has an envelope showing that it is rather different from all other species.

Measures of Locomotor Activities

Our summaries depend upon attempts to define the degree to which individual locomotor activities, habitat utilizations, and dietary preferences are similar or different for each species. Let us first examine locomotor-related activities.

Rather than characterizing four-legged movement as simply quadrupedalism, we distinguish a variety of different forms of four-legged movement. These include slow quadrupedal movement, fast quadrupedal movement (scurrying), running leaping, and climbing. We use several categories because, although quadrupedalism is a useful broad descriptor, it seems clear that there are various ways in which four-footed movements may be carried out. On anatomical grounds, there are biomechanically different ways to engage in what so many authors have classified as generalized quadrupedalism (Oxnard 1983).

For example, slow quadrupedal walking is different from quadrupedal climbing in the consequences for the forelimb in the latter. Quadrupedal running with continuous movement into and out of regular leaps has been frequently described in the literature on prosimian locomotion (e.g., see Bearder 1974; Charles-Dominique 1977; Crompton 1980). We expect that in future formal gait analyses, running leaping will be shown to be a distinct movement. Scurrying is a good descriptor for the fast quadrupedal movement of perhaps the more conservative of living primates, such as *Microcebus murinus* and *Galago demidovii*. At present, however, its biomechanical implications are unclear and its relationships with other quadrupedal gait patterns are unknown.

All of these locomotor characteristics are affected by overall size, or scale. Scaling factors, particularly the effects of stride length on maximum speed in various formally defined gaits, are likely to be of great relevance to our understanding of many of these quadrupedal gaits in prosimians (see Taylor, Schmidt-Nielsen, and Raab 1970; Alexander 1977; Hildebrand 1980). Little attempt has been made so far to analyze prosimian gaits in this manner, though Rollinson and Martin (1980) briefly discuss diagonal gaits in prosimians. There is much room for further research here.

Undoubtedly these activities often grade into one another in specific species. For instance, slow horizontal quadrupedal movement presumably merges into quadrupedal climbing in some species and into fast quadrupedal movement (scurrying) in others. This last, in turn, may well merge into quadrupedal running and thence into quadrupedal running with leaping. However, we have resisted the temptation to place each of these categories as a component in a single axis of quadrupedalism because, in other species, it is entirely possible that these do not form continuous grades of activity.

Such differences are evident in the monkeys. Thus, in New World monkeys, the anatomical correlates of "generalized quadrupedalism" seem to be graded toward anatomies related to other more extreme activities of primates—for examples, arboreal suspensory acrobatics. In Old World monkeys, in contrast, the anatomical correlates of generalized quadrupedalism appear not to grade toward the more extreme primate modes at all, but to be correlated specifically to different forms of quadrupedalism itself (Oxnard 1983).

Pertaining to the species studied in this book, though some movements may well grade into one another as described above (e.g., as in lemurs), in other species they may not do so. For instance, the slow quadrupedal movement of lorisines does not grade into quadrupedal scurrying, or into running with leaping. These are almost certainly species differences that will be found on further study to relate to gait-pattern/stride-length/speed relationships. For the present, the raw behavioral information is extensive enough to allow a general assessment of the degree to which each type of four-footed activity is performed by most of the species concerned.

A second locomotor activity is that covered by the simple term "leaping." Though originally characterized as "leaping" (e.g., Mollison 1910) and more recently by the more specialized prosimian term "vertical clinging and leaping" (e.g., Napier and Napier [1967], who immediately broadened the category to include almost all forms of prosimian leaping), it is now clear that different forms of leaping have quite different biomechanical implications (Oxnard 1983).

We have chosen to distinguish running leaping from falling leaping (such as described by Charles-Dominique 1977, for *Galago elegantulus*) in which movement tends to be achieved as much by gravity as by hindlimb propulsion. And we have chosen to distinguish each of these from crouching leaping. This involves the body being held with flexed limbs and, at least momentarily, appressed to the substrate before take-off. This, in turn, we have distinguished from ricochetal leaping, which has only relatively minor involvement of the forelimbs and only a short interval between landing from one leap and subsequent take-off. The latter feature has, for example, obvious biomechanical and physiological implications in terms of mechanical cyclicity and elastic storage of energy by tendons.

Undoubtedly other components of leaping exist and could be included. Oxnard (1983) has defined special take-off, mid-air, and landing positions. Yet, though considerable information is available about these components for some of the species, current behavioral descriptions do not allow their use for all of the animals concerned. Accordingly, such further detailed breakdown must be deferred until more information is available.

Again, as with the various forms of quadrupedalism, it would have been possible to arrange these types of leaping as individual measures in a single scale of leaping. In such a scheme falling leaping might perhaps be thought of as least specialized and ricochetal leaping as most specialized. There is a distinct likelihood, however, that though such a spectrum might be a true description for some species (for example, some galagos), in other species (for example, some tarsiers) this is not so. We have thus kept each form of leaping separate in the evaluations that we have made from the field data.

Insufficient data are available for us to include a category of suspensory activity, never mind to subdivide it. We know that it is an important component of movement and posture. It is especially related to particular habitats. It is important for certain dietary choices. Oxnard discusses in detail suspension by upper limbs (1983), showing how it can arise not only from arm-swinging, the locomotor pattern that most frequently springs to mind when the word "suspension" is used, but also from numerous other activities. These include many activities that are obviously locomotor, such as, hanging before drops, pulling up, vertical climbing, horizontal upside-down walking, certain types of landing after leaps, elastic recoil of branches in many locomotor activities, and so on. But they also include many postures, such as hanging, support from above in many forms of sitting, lateral support in branch crotches generating tensile forces, and so on. And they include many totally non-locomotor activities as in foraging, that is, pulling in with one limb branches containing foods, supporting from above or laterally while foraging with one limb, and so on; nest making, i.e., pulling in elastic branches; nursing, i.e., tensile limb forces in infants; and special play and escape activities. There are many other activities that may result in tensile forces in upper limbs.

The measures detailed here will easily allow us to add one or more suspensory activity variables to the overall data when the information becomes available for all species. It is clearly a most important activity category. We hope that this discussion will stimulate such research.

Measures of Habitat Utilization

In a similar way, we describe aspects of several different elements of the habitat: canopy, undergrowth, horizontal substrates, vertical substrates, small diameter supports (twigs and foliage), and large diameter supports (branches). These parameters are not retained as scales or spectra (e.g., a scale from canopy to undergrowth, from horizontal to vertical substrates, from small diameter supports—twigs and foliage—to large diameter ones—branches) for much the same reason that the forms of locomotion are not.

As Rose (1974) has observed for the locomotor types, observations tend to be polarized along these spectra and thus tend to fall into modes. A species that spends much time in the undergrowth of tropical forest (say, a tarsier) hardly ever meets up with a canopy-dweller (say, a slow loris) in the same forest.

This is the same problem that we have just described for the locomotor parameters. Spectra in these characteristics do, of course, exist for some species, but they do not, or are inappropriate, for others. The biomechanical consequences of moving between vertical supports may be clearly very different from those of moving between horizontal ones, given the usual pattern of spacing of the two support types (roughly, discontinuous versus continuous) and the body size of most prosimians.

We must also observe that the way that we have been forced to organize the data, based upon the information available, does not mean that these pairs of characteristics are necessarily complementary. A finding of 30 percent of horizontal supports involved in locomotion does not necessarily imply 70 percent of vertical ones; 20 percent of canopy time does not necessarily mean 80 percent in the undergrowth. There are other possibilities about which we have only little information, yet their existence says that we must keep these parameters separate from one another.

Measures of Dietary Preferences

Even in what some might think was a fairly clear matter, dietary preference, many early descriptions have been overly simplistic, emphasizing broad categories such as herbivory and carnivory. We have chosen to diversify the range of diet choices to include, separately, parameters such as (a) fruit, (b) gums and nectar, (c) leaves, buds, and flowers, and (d) animal materials (invertebrates and vertebrates). In particular animals, such dietary items may form part of a spectrum, for example, fruits, flowers, buds, and leaves in generalists. In specialists, on the other hand, these categories might be mutually exclusive. Yet we must be careful. In some animal groups the two categories—specialists and generalists—may truly exist; in others, there may be a single spectrum that goes from extreme generalists to extreme specialists.

For all of these reasons, therefore, as for activity and habitat, we have kept the various dietary parameters as separate as we could. Should these more complex interactions exist, we hope that they would be revealed by the secondary analyses that we apply to the raw data.

Dietary choices other than those described here do exist (for example, roots and shoots). And new information about associations between unusual elements of the diet is being discovered (for example, the dietary importance, for some species, of fallen fruit infested with invertebrates [Redford, Bouchardet da Fonseca, and Lacher 1984]). At present, however, such information is too scanty for us to be able to provide quantitative estimates for them.

Interactions among
Activities, Habitats, and Diets

Clearly, there will sometimes be strong correlations among the locomotor activities of an animal, the characteristics of the arboreal zone that it inhabits, and the dietary items which it chooses. For example, slow quadrupedalism occurs in a milieu of large horizontal branches that are closely spaced. Climbing can less readily occur there. In contrast, at any other than the smallest body size, regular quadrupedalism is unlikely in a zone with small, densely packed, irregularly oriented supports. Dietary preferences are likely also associated with these characteristics at some times and for some species. (But we note that this will not be true for all sites where an animal might be observed).

Even for anatomical characteristics there will be heavy correlations for some creatures. Not only might this involve a simple anatomical feature such as gross body size, but more complex ones such as the relative length of limbs, and the degree of habitual flexure of the limb with respect to the axial skeleton. Each of these, for instance, might be related in a particular species to the size, orientation, and density of supports in the normal habitat. This is well seen, for instance, in the polarization in gross body proportions noted by McArdle (1978, 1981) for the Lorisinae. Another example is in habitual leapers, for which leap trajectory has been suggested as related to the density of supports in the environment (Charles-Dominique 1977).

On the other hand, the correlation of particular forest zones with particular kinds of locomotion cannot always be assumed. Climbing can equally well occur in the undergrowth or the canopy, all other things being equal. Any association of arboreal zone and locomotor mode (see, e.g., Crompton 1983) can, at the present state of our knowledge, be examined only for close relatives with at least qualitatively similar anatomies. A particular species may, of course, be confined to the canopy, or to the undergrowth, and if this is the case, forest layer will be reflected in its locomotor anatomy. The anatomy in turn will relate to its potential locomotor repertoire. And, this, in further sequence, will be associated with its dietary needs, and, through the dispersion of its staple food stuff and the support type on which the food is located, with the type of supports that it regularly utilizes.

These examples illustrate that, though in some cases we would expect heavy correlations among the different activity, environment, and dietary variables, in other cases we do not.

In the first instance, therefore, we have deemed it important not to assume that a particular habitat is unequivocally associated with a particular movement pattern or a special dietary choice, but to hold the activity, habitat, and dietary variables as independent until proven otherwise. Almost certainly the final disposition will prove to be that there are different degrees of dependence among the activities, the habitats, and the diets for different species. What is a high level of dependence in one species may be intermediate in another and vanishingly small in a third. But these independencies and dependencies should not be assumed a priori. They are best tested and allowed for in the secondary, multivariate statistical handling of the data.

The constraints which will most likely govern the dependence or independence of locomotor activities, habitats, and diets in a given species are those we have just discussed. In addition, however, other factors may be involved. Thus, energetic constraints, marked in a species living in a seasonally marginal environment, might sometimes produce greater dependence upon locomotion and habitat in subtropical regions. It is possible that a greater independence might be expected in a more predictable though diverse tropical/equatorial zone. Even here, however, the matter is complex. In tropical zones, the opposite might be the case for specialists. More diverse habitats have a greater resource partitioning, more niche overlaps, and a larger number of specialists. And we must be especially careful to recognize the different types of tropical forest and not simplistically to lump them together.

Such complexities may apply to many species. Greater niche diversification might result in certain species having diets that place limitations on behavioral flexibility. But it is also possible that there could be a selective advantage for a more specialized diet in a more predictable habitat. It is not clear which of these might apply, for instance, to species such as *Loris tardigradus* and *Arctocebus*.

We are far from being able to evaluate the general characteristics of energetic constraints on locomotor behavior and habitat selection. Indeed, some earlier views on particular dietary/energy/locomotor interactions are now being seriously questioned (for example, the debate about caecotrophy in *Lepilemur*; see Hladik 1979).

An initial naiveté must, therefore, be expected in our data. We must largely limit ourselves to recognizing, for each animal group, locomotor activities as a set of different movement patterns that may or may not merge into one another. We must limit ourselves to seeing the habitat as containing a series of functional milieus that may or may not link with one another. We must view dietary choices as a series of different commodities that may or may not be mutually exclusive. In the first instance, we shall not assume that such variables grade one into another, or are especially associated with one another.

Interactions within Activities, Habitats, and Diets

Given some degree of morphological similarity for a group of animals, the biomechanical consequences of different activities may suggest that similarity in one movement (e.g., leaping) implies similarity in another (e.g., climbing). This may well be so in some forms; for instance, lorises that do not leap, climb well. The finding that angwantibos also do not leap implies, in this case correctly, that they, too, climb well. However, such internal correlations within the activity variables will not hold for other species.

In the same way it cannot be assumed that the habitat utilization parameters that we have selected are necessarily either highly dependent on each other or highly independent. And we also have, at this stage of our investigations, no ability to predict overall which diets are associated with which others or not, in any given group of animals. Thus, just as we do not necessarily assume correlations among the activity, habitat, and dietary categories, neither do we assume them within these categories.

Let us look at some examples of this for habitat variables. In a study of two *Galago* species in the bushveldt of South Africa reported by Crompton, it was found that there was indeed a statistically significant correlation between height and alignment of support. Supports used higher up tended in general to be more horizontal, those used lower down, more vertical. In the simple bushveldt environment this could easily be related to the "flattening out," with height, of the crowns of *Acacia karoo* and *Acacia tortilis* trees. These trees were dominant in the study sites both in terms of number and because they provided the gums that, at least in winter, were the staple of the bushbabies' diet. There was also a weaker tendency for supports used higher up to be smaller. A similar observation might be expected in the dipterocarp forests of Borneo, for example, where *Shorea, Dipterocarpus*, and other canopy and emergent species tend to have wide, horizontally based crowns.

In other cases, however, branches in the peripheral canopy may be small, but their orientation very variable. A species that utilizes the peripheral crowns a good deal, as in fruit-gathering or insect-feeding, will encounter many small supports, but not necessarily largely horizontal ones. In some tree species (in tropical forest, usually those exploiting small forest clearings), the height of supports and support orientation are independent. In others (such as *Acacia*), however, they are dependent. Though degrees of independence of such parameters do exist and can sometimes be estimated, it is highly likely that correlations will be quite different in different parts of the spectrum of environments.

Some special interactions between variables

There may well be special degrees of dependence between habitat parameters and locomotor activities. For instance, a falling leap onto a large horizontal branch has a quite different biomechanical implication than does a falling leap onto a mass of small horizontal twigs. A large-bodied animal like *Presbytis* or *Ateles* would be ill-advised to carry out the former, but could readily perform the latter. On the other hand, an animal the size of *Galago crassicaudatus* would not be injured by a falling leap onto a large branch. Crompton has seen *G. crassicaudatus* recover within a minute or two from a fall of twenty feet or more onto the ground.

Biomechanical considerations, therefore, additionally complicate the degrees of interdependence of our variables. Variables that are heavily correlated in a large species may be independent in a small species.

Again, the implications of living in a given part of the habitat may vary depending upon the habitual locomotor repertoire of a species. Thus, *Loris tardigradus*, a "slow climber," would be subject to different aspects of support/locomotor interactions than would, in an equivalent habitat, a "scurry leaper" such as *Galago demidovii* or *Microcebus*.

Further, the dietary habits and locomotor repertoire of a species sometimes do determine the subunits of a broad arboreal zone that it may occupy, as well as the type of activity/habitat interactions that it encounters. For example, *Galago demidovii*, elsewhere found in foliage tangles in the undergrowth (Oates 1984), occurs in Gabon in the low canopy, in "liane curtains" (Charles-Dominique 1977), which provide an abundance of small vertical supports, similar in characteristics to the supports in the undergrowth.

A second special interaction relates to what is "perceived" by the animals as a result of their lifestyles. It is not the absolute abundance in the environment of a particular kind of support which is important, but the supports a given animal "sees" or "uses" because of its particular dietary habits and locomotor repertoire. In the South African study cited earlier, another common tree, *Combretum imberbwe*, seemed primarily to provide either large horizontal boughs, which could be visualized as "arboreal motorways," or relatively small vertical shoots, through which latter one could visualize a small saltatory animal moving rapidly. However, *Galago crassicaudatus*, the bushbaby species present in the area with abundant *Combretum imberbwe*, while successfully using the "arboreal motorways" for quadrupedalism, leapt for only a fifth of observations and only very rarely between verticals. The other species, on the other hand, used leaps between verticals quite commonly, and walked only a little. Vertical shoots were not, then, part of the "umwelt" of *G. crassicaudatus*.

And, finally, we must emphasize that, although a tree may be common and its support types numerically abundant in the environment, if the animal's major foodstuff is not located on that tree, the animal will be much less inclined to use it. This was indeed the case with *Combretum* for *Galago crassicaudatus,* which seldom utilized its saps, but instead fed on *Acacia* gums and therefore spent a "disproportionate" amount of time in *Acacia,* despite the absolutely high frequency of *Combretum.*

It is frequently noted in the ecological literature that resources are often used in proportions that differ significantly from what is available in the habitat. This is, indeed, one test of habitat partitioning (e.g., Lieberman 1982). That is what we are noting here, since trees are a spatial resource.

We can expect then, as we have emphasized repeatedly, varying degrees of dependence and independence both within and among the activity, habitat-utilization, and dietary-preference parameters in the different species. For most, the parameters will be neither largely independent nor largely dependent. Of course, in some cases the degrees of interdependence may be extreme. *Hapalemur griseus,* living in bamboo groves in Madagascar, must encounter vertical supports very frequently, and its locomotion must be heavily constrained by their availability. The subspecies *H. griseus alaotrensis,* which is confined to the reedbeds of the Malagasy lake Alaotra, must encounter even fewer supports that are not vertically oriented.

In each and every combination, the "activity dimensions" will have a wide range of different correlations with the "habitat utilizations" and the "dietary choices." No alternative exists at this stage but for us to present the raw data as the separate descriptors, and to look for correlations among and between them at a later stage of the study.

3 Activity, Habitat, and Diet for Each Species

Fig. 3.1. *Arctocebus calabarensis* (after a photograph by Napier)

Lorisinae

Arctocebus calabarensis, the angwantibo

The angwantibo (figs. 3.1 and 3.2) has been observed in the field by Jewell and Oates (1969) in Nigeria and by Charles-Dominique (1979) at Makoukou, Gabon. Summaries of available data on diet are provided by Hladik (1979) and on locomotion by Walker (1979). No videotape or film was available to us.

Quantified summaries of several aspects of support use and habitat use are provided by Charles-Dominique from his Gabon study, and these generally agree with the observations of Jewell and Oates. The angwantibo seems to be limited largely to the undergrowth, usually below 5 meters in primary forest, where it prefers the densely packed supports available in regenerating tree-fall zones. Alone among the lorisines, it is apparently incapable of supporting itself on supports of over 20 centimeters in diameter. It has relatively small hands and seems to prefer small supports, commonly using verticals, largely lianes. In comparison with *Loris*, the angwantibo is distinguished by stratum, by greater use of vertical supports, and by limitation to supports of small diameter only. Its diet is more restricted to in-

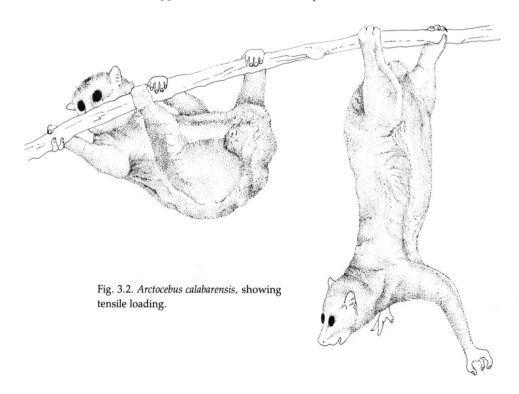

Fig. 3.2. *Arctocebus calabarensis,* showing tensile loading.

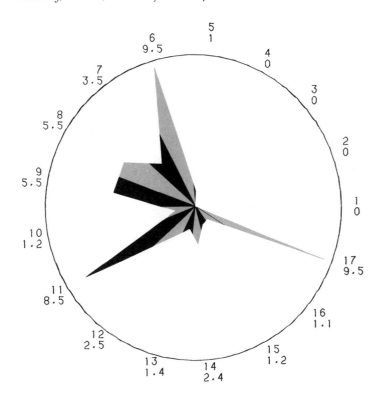

Fig. 3.3. Profile of *Arctocebus calabarensis*

vertebrate prey, and it consumes species unpalatable to *Loris*, such as hairy caterpillars.

There are no adequate descriptions of the angwantibo's slow quadrupedalism. From evidence of support use and available descriptions, climbing seems much more frequent than walking.

True suspension, both in postures and during climbing, does not seem to be overly frequent; but because of the angwantibo's locomotor habits, we imagine that tensile loading of the musculoskeletal system (sensu Oxnard 1983) would be a common consequence of normal locomotion.

Figure 3.3 shows the polar coordinate plot of the totality of the raw data for these species. It indicates that the animals have very high values for time spent in the undergrowth, in climbing, and in eating animal dietary items, as well as considerable values for horizontal and vertical supports, as compared with all other parameters.

Loris tardigradus, the slender loris

The slender loris (figs. 3.4 and 3.5) has been observed in the wild by Subramoniam (1956) in Sri Lanka and by Petter and Hladik (1979) at Polunnarawa, Sri Lanka. Reviews of diet and locomotion are presented by Hladik (1979) and by Walker (1979). No quantitative data on locomotion appear to have been published, and no videotape or film records were available to us.

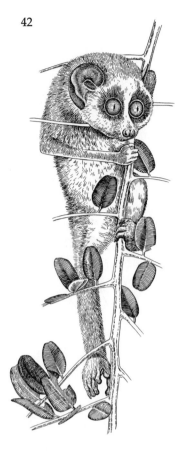

Fig. 3.4. *Loris tardigradus* (after a photograph by Napier and Walker)

Notwithstanding the paucity of primary sources of information, it seems clear that *Loris* fills a similar niche in Asia to that of *Arctocebus* in West Africa. *Loris* is, in other words, a slow climber in undergrowth and lianes. Its diet, arboreal zone, and support usage, however, seem rather more generalized. It feeds less exclusively on invertebrates. It is found in a wider variety of arboreal zones. It appears to use larger supports more readily than does *Arctocebus*, and it makes use of a wider variety of support orientations than *Arctocebus*, which possibly displays a greater preference for liane curtains in regenerating tree-fall zones.

The more generalized activity patterns of *Loris* may relate to the absence of confamilial competitors in its Asian environments. In West Africa, in particular, *Arctocebus* may be competing with *Galago demidovii* as a small insectivorous primate inhabiting liane curtains and foliage tangles. Elsewhere than at Makoukou, Jewell and Oates (1969) have recorded *G. demidovii* as inhabiting the undergrowth; Charles-Dominique notes it most often in the canopy and records *Arctocebus* almost exclusively in the undergrowth. Morphological differences between the two species, such as the relatively smaller hands of *Arctocebus*, must act as determinants in habitat selection. Yet, at the same time, the morphological differences must themselves be, to a large extent, consequences of, or coeval with, the activity specializations.

As with *Arctocebus*, and as emphasized by Subramoniam's diagrams, locomotor and postural activity is likely to involve frequent tensile loading of the limbs. Subramoniam and Petter and Hladik note that *Loris* frequently engages in the "cantilever" maneuver or "flag-posture" typical of several small lorisids and cheirogaleines (e.g., Martin 1972; Crompton 1984). This movement is figured in Oxnard (1983) and is likely to result in high bending moments about the ankle and foot joints and high tensile forces in sections of long distal segments. It is closely related to insect-catching behavior.

Figure 3.6 shows the polar coordinate plot of the totality of the raw data for this species. Like the plot for the angwantibo, it shows high values for climbing and animal dietary items. It also shows fairly high values for both canopy and undergrowth, with the predominance on smaller supports.

Fig. 3.5. *Loris tardigradus,* showing slow quadrepedal climbing.

Fig. 3.6. Profile of *Loris tardigradus*

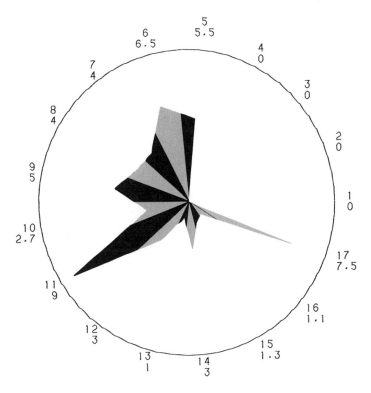

Fig. 3.7. *Perodicticus potto*, showing spiraling movement.

Perodicticus potto, the potto

The potto (fig. 3.7) has been observed in the wild by Walker (1969) in Uganda, by Kingdon (1971) in Kenya and Uganda, and by Oates (most recently in 1984) in Sierra Leone (Tiwai Island) and Nigeria (Bendel State: Sapoba and Okomu Forest Reserve). But the most extensive observations remain those of Charles-Dominique (1977) at Makoukou, Gabon. The reviews by Walker (1979) and Hladik (1979) are also helpful. Film of captive *Perodicticus* was made available by Walker and additional videotaping and x-ray cinematography on captive specimens have been carried out by Crompton. Quantitative data on locomotion are generally lacking.

The activity of *Perodicticus* has previously been regarded as generally similar to that of *Nycticebus*. Field observations that it lives predominantly in the canopy have been confirmed by radio-tracking. Charles-Dominique and more particularly Oates observe that it prefers larger supports to foliage, but Charles-Dominique writes that its means of progression from tree to tree by moving out into the periphery of the canopy and then bridging over into the foliage of the next tree, ensures that it encounters a wide variety of supports of different sizes and orientations. Oates stresses a similarity of locomotion and ecology of *Galago crassicaudatus*.

According to Oates, gum is a much more important dietary element in *Perodicticus* than has previously been thought, and it may well be its predominant element in seasons when fruit is lacking. Pending additional information, however, we have conservatively rated fruits as higher than gums in the dietary estimates.

Given that gum is an important constituent in the diet of *Perodicticus*, Oates sees many of the locomotor adaptations that have been regarded by Walker (1969), among others, as adaptations to stealth, relating rather to the search for gums on tree trunks and large branches. Since, as Crompton reports for *Galago crassicaudatus* (1980, 1984), large gum sources are most frequently located on the trunks of trees and the undersides of major branches, *Perodicticus* is particularly adapted for suspensory locomotion and posture (a predilection also noted in Oxnard 1983). In Crompton's observations from film, and following Walker's 1969 reports, *Perodicticus*, of all primates, seems to move quite readily underneath branches, spiraling round them at trunk/branch nodes or at branch points. The forelimbs of *Perodicticus* are heavily involved in most propulsion. Its limbs are used in rather abducted positions in both climbing and walking.

There is, as Oates notes, no "floating" phase in its gait, although Walker is incorrect in stating that three limbs are always involved in movement, if by that is meant that three limbs are *always* in contact with the support. Walking and "running" are both features of *Perodicticus* locomotion. Slow quadrupedal climbing seems, however, to be the dominant element (probably unlike *Nycticebus*).

Different anatomical elements of *Perodicticus* must be highly subject to tensile loading during the course of its normal locomotion. However, as previously explained, our ignorance of this as a factor in so many others of the prosimians prevents us from including it as a major parameter. Certainly its climbing, "spiraling," and "bridging" behavior make it likely that its musculoskeletal system is highly adapted to bearing tension.

It seems, then, that the niche and activity of *Perodicticus* is not quite as similar to that of *Nycticebus* as generally thought. Our lack of knowledge of *Nycticebus* at present prevents clarification of the extent and reasons for the differences.

Figure 3.8 shows the polar coordinate plot of the totality of the raw data for this species. In this case the emphasis on climbing of the lorisines is still obvious, as is lesser but still large use of horizontal and vertical supports. But the diet is different, no longer a predominance of animal items but rather fruit. This last was beginning to be evident in the plot for *Loris*.

Nycticebus coucang, the slow loris

Very little information is available on the behavior of *Nycticebus* (fig. 3.9). Walker summarized some earlier notes (1979), and Dykyj made a study of captive *Nycticebus* (1980). Barrett has made observations in Peninsular Malaysia, and Crompton, in Sabah. Hladik (1979) reporting Elliot and Elliot (1967) is our main source of information on diet. Crompton has recorded *Nycticebus* locomotion on videotape.

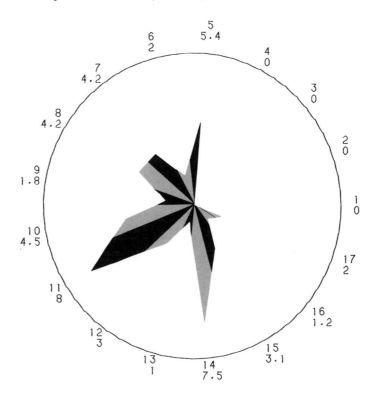

Fig. 3.8. Profile of *Perodicticus potto*

Fig. 3.9. *Nycticebus coucang*
(after a photograph by Walker)

From published information, *Nycticebus* seems almost exclusively a canopy dweller under undisturbed conditions, and only comes to lower levels in regions such as fruit plantations. According to Barrett, the slow loris in Peninsular Malaysia *frequently* uses the understory (personal communication). Until Barrett's observations are published or confirmed, we will here retain the more conservative view supported by Crompton's observations in Sabah (Sepilok Forest Reserve).

As with *Perodicticus*, *Nycticebus* favors larger supports, but since Dykyj found that it favored 2-centimeter supports over 4-centimeter supports in discontinuous networks, and since the animal has not been recorded to our knowledge on tree trunks, we feel it is less specialized in this direction than *Perodicticus*. Dykyj's quantitative data and Crompton's limited field observations indicate a greater affinity for horizontal supports than *Perodicticus*. Since in primary forest in Borneo at least, common trees such as *Shorea* tend to have rather "flattened" wide bases to their crowns, it is likely that an abundance of continuous horizontal or near horizontal pathways exist within the lower parts of the continuous canopy, and therefore also likely that habitat structure produces a bias toward horizontal support use in canopy-living animals. Dykyj's data are again supported by Crompton's observations from videotapes that suspensory locomotion and suspensory postures are not very common in *Nycticebus*, and suspensory locomotion in particular is considerably less common than in *Perodicticus*. Dykyj found that diagonal couplets and trotting were the most common gait patterns. Crompton has seen considerably more walking than climbing in his field observations.

Nycticebus climbing is slower and less "confident" than that of *Perodicticus*; in particular, forelimb involvement is less evident. Limbs appear to be used in a less abducted position than in *Perodicticus*. Suspensory postures like those of *Galago crassicaudatus* rely more heavily upon the hindlimb than do those of *Perodicticus*.

Diet in *Nycticebus* is largely unknown. Elliot and Elliot (1967) suggest that the *Nycticebus* diet is heavily insectivorous, yet, like *Arctocebus*, includes items repugnant to most insectivorous primates. But Hladik (1967) believes that *Nycticebus'* large body size indicates that fruit must be a major component of the diet. The publication of Barrett's work should illuminate this.

The locomotor and probably dietary differences between the two large-bodied lorisines are consistent with each other. Anatomically, the apparent greater relative forelimb mass of *Perodicticus* and its greater specialization in loss of the second digit, also seem consistent with our findings. It seems to us that Oates (1984) is correct in referring many of *Perodicticus'* anatomical specializations to a heavily, if seasonally, gummivorous diet, although the comparison to *Galago crassicaudatus* can be stretched too far. *Nycticebus* seems to lack these particular specializations but, overall, behaves in a sim-

Fig. 3.10. Profile of *Nycticebus coucang*

ilar way to the potto. In terms of the still absolutely high frequency of climbing behavior, tensile loading (as noted in Oxnard 1983) must be frequent in *Nycticebus*, but not as frequent or as great as in *Perodicticus*.

Figure 3.10 shows the polar coordinate plot of the totality of the raw data for this species. Climbing and slow quadrupedalism, small and large supports, and vertical and horizontal supports in the canopy are all well represented. Diet includes both fruit and animal products.

Galaginae

Galago garnettii, the small thick-tailed bushbaby

We are making a species-level distinction between the large-bodied *Galago crassicaudatus* of Southern Africa, previously known as *G. crassicaudatus umbrosus*, and the small-bodied form from East Africa previously known as *G. crassicaudatus garnettii*. They are probably two separate species and, although it is not our intention to engage in taxonomic discussions, we refer to them as such by these convenient names.

Galago garnettii has been studied in the field at Diani and Gedi, Kenya, by Nash (1983) and by Harcourt (personal communication). We rely entirely on these authors and on notes by Walker (1979) and Kingdon (1971). A short film sequence of *G. garnettii* was provided by Walker. Nash's report has only limited amounts of quantified information on the locomotion of *G. garnettii*, but enough information is available to indicate that locomotion is rather different in the smaller species.

The smaller species appears to exhibit a greater affinity for larger supports and for horizontal supports than does *Galago crassicaudatus*. This may be a consequence of sympatry of *G. garnettii* and *G. zanzibaricus*. *G. crassicaudatus* was not studied in sympatry with *G. senegalensis* in the South African studies (sympatry between these two species is rare). It may also, however, be an artifact of differences in method and sample-size between Nash's and Crompton's studies. And yet again, it may be due to differences in structure in the two forest habitats between South African riparian woodland and Kenyan coastal woodland.

Galago garnettii is most clearly distinguished from *G. crassicaudatus* in its greater use of hopping, ricochetal leaping, and crouching leaping (Nash 1983; personal communications, Walker and Harcourt). The former makes less use of walking and climbing than the latter. This would be consistent with its more frugivorous and insectivorous and much less gummivorous diet, together with appropriate foraging strategy given its body size and more stable environment (see Crompton 1980, 1984).

For a galagine, we would expect that tensile loading would be moderate, and based largely upon the tensions created during take-off and landing in leaping by factors such as posture and branch whiplash.

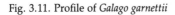

Fig. 3.11. Profile of *Galago garnettii*

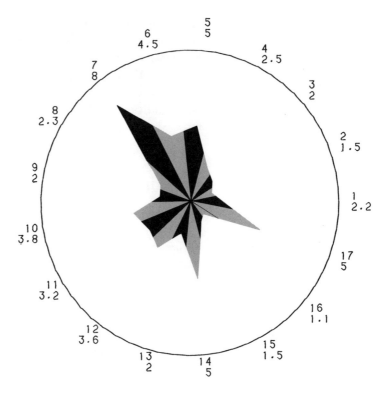

Figure 3.11 shows the polar coordinate plot of the totality of the raw data for this species. The plot emphasizes high values only for horizontal supports. There are somewhat lesser values for ricochetal leaping. There are small values (but still distinguishable from the remaining variables) for canopy, large supports, climbing, and fruit and animal items.

Galago crassicaudatus, the thick-tailed or greater bushbaby

The thick-tailed bushbaby (figs. 3.12 and 3.13) has been studied in the field by Clarke (1978), Harcourt (1980), and by Crompton (1980, 1983, and 1984) at Louis Trichardt in South Africa. Crompton has concentrated mostly on aspects relevant to the present study, and has also made videotapes of the species under both captive and field conditions. For this reason, the plots for this species and for *Galago senegalensis* are highly reliable.

This species lives in riparian *Acacia* woodland in Southern Africa. Its major dietary constituents are the gum of *Acacia karoo* and arthropod prey (although fruits may partly replace gums elsewhere). Gums become almost the exclusive food in the dry seasons. Crompton has shown that the slow quadrupedal locomotion of *Galago crassicaudatus* is an integral part of an adaptation allowing an almost exclusively gum diet in an unstable environment in seasons when arthropod prey are scarce. According to Oates (1984), *Perodicticus* locomotion is comparable to that of *G. crassicaudatus* in

Fig. 3.12. *Galago crassicaudatus* (redrawn after Estey), showing tensile loading.

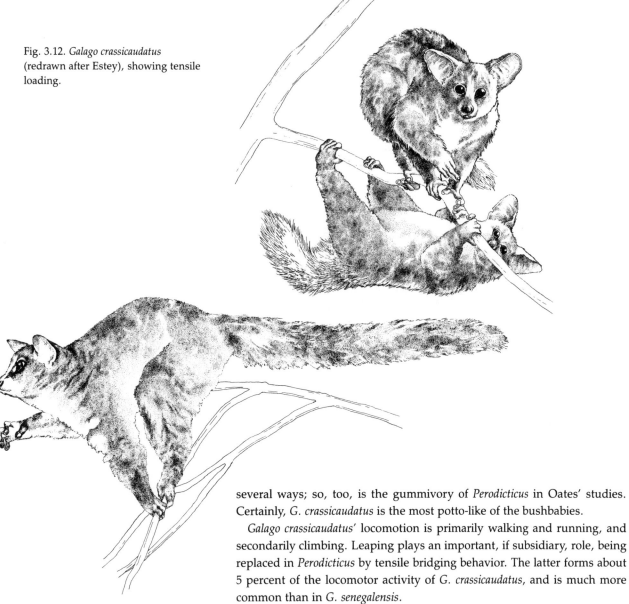

Fig. 3.13. *Galago crassicaudatus* (after a photograph by Bearder), showing the transition from running to leaping.

several ways; so, too, is the gummivory of *Perodicticus* in Oates' studies. Certainly, *G. crassicaudatus* is the most potto-like of the bushbabies.

Galago crassicaudatus' locomotion is primarily walking and running, and secondarily climbing. Leaping plays an important, if subsidiary, role, being replaced in *Perodicticus* by tensile bridging behavior. The latter forms about 5 percent of the locomotor activity of *G. crassicaudatus*, and is much more common than in *G. senegalensis*.

Spiraling movement around supports during climbing is sometimes observed in *Galago crassicaudatus*, but by no means as commonly as in *Perodicticus*. Four-limb suspension during posture is seen in about 4 percent of postural observations made in *G. crassicaudatus*. Descending vertical or near vertical supports head down is in fact less common in the large-bodied *G. crassicaudatus* than in the small-bodied *G. senegalensis*. In both galagos, standing postures are much more common than clinging postures in gum feeding. Thus, *Perodicticus'* specializations are only partially echoed in *G. crassicaudatus*, which is, of course, a galago, if a rather unusual one.

Leaping in *Galago crassicaudatus* is, in frequency, dominated by leaps made during sequences of running, and serves to shorten routes or cross short gaps. Falling leaps, in which foliage is used to break the fall, are also observed in the context of crossing between tree canopies, and form the second most common type of leap. Ricochetal leaping and hopping are rare events, and they usually occur during play or escape. This may relate to energy costs, or to the fact that the forelimb-first landing style of *G. crassicaudatus* could be creating unacceptably high compression on the forelimb at its larger body weight.

Walking and running in *Galago crassicaudatus* employ a variety of gait patterns, but again, unlike the potto, running regularly includes a floating phase. The limbs are not held abducted as they are in both *Nycticebus* and *Perodicticus*. Thus, while strong dietary similarities may have led to a degree of convergence between *G. crassicaudatus* and *Perodicticus potto*—and their similar foraging habits may be the reason why their ranges hardly ever overlap, if indeed, they overlap at all (see maps in Kingdon 1971)—there are strong differences in locomotion which emphasize the underlying locomotor integrity of the two taxonomic groups in the Lorisidae.

Tension-bearing is undoubtedly produced by bridging or foliage-crossing behavior, common in both the potto and the greater galago. But, tension-generating cantilevering (or the flag posture) related to insect feeding, and descending behavior are actually more common in the small, less gummivorous species than in *Galago crassicaudatus*. Suspensory postures overall are more common in play than in feeding in *G. crassicaudatus*.

Figure 3.14 shows the polar coordinate plot of the totality of the raw data for this species. It demonstrates very well the high values for canopy and gums and nectar, with considerable values for climbing and slow quadrupedalism, with lesser values still for various leaping modes and animal items. These are all as compared with very low values for other variables.

Galago alleni, Allen's bushbaby

Galago alleni (figs. 3.15 and 3.16) has been studied in the field by Charles-Dominique (1977) at Makoukou in Gabon and also has been observed by Jewell and Oates (1969) in Nigeria. Hladik (1979) and Walker (1979) provide reviews of diet and locomotion. No video or film records were available.

Charles-Dominique's study of *Galago alleni* at Makoukou raises many questions and further field study is necessary. This animal's specializations seem extreme, if Charles-Dominique's results, based on a fairly small sample, are representative. He describes it as a forest-floor dweller, with high affinity for vertical supports, and having a predominantly ricochetal locomotor style, but infrequently quadrupedal. Not surprisingly, it has a locomotor profile that most resembles that of tarsiers. Its diet is apparently primarily fallen fruit; its body weight is the same as, or a little less than, that of *G. senegalensis*, which is primarily insectivorous (although partially gummivorous) and considerably less specialized.

Fig. 3.14. Profile of *Galago crassicaudatus*

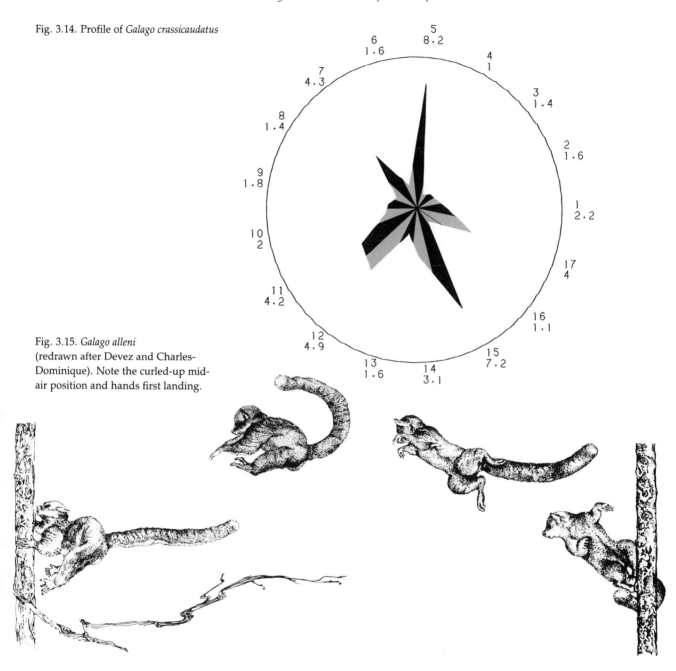

Fig. 3.15. *Galago alleni* (redrawn after Devez and Charles-Dominique). Note the curled-up mid-air position and hands first landing.

The above is a curious combination of features and either the data are unrepresentative or something very unusual exists here. It is possible that sample size is part of the problem. Charles-Dominique describes locomotion as "almost exclusively" leaping between small vertical supports near ground level, yet elsewhere says that *Galago alleni* also displays "great prowess" at running. It is possible, but unlikely, that the two locomotor styles are combined in this way. None of the other outstanding prosimian leapers—*G. senegalensis*, the indriids, or the tarsiers—are good runners. At

Fig. 3.16. *Galago alleni*
(after photographs by Devez)

high speed it makes more physiological and biomechanical "sense" for them to leap.

Charles-Dominique provided photographs and descriptions of the standard ricochetal leap in *Galago alleni*. The body is not curled up in midflight, as in the leaps of some tarsiers and *G. senegalensis*, but horizontal, as with *G. demidovii* and *Microcebus*. The tail is actively used to control body position. Initial contact on landing is made with the forelimbs, quite unlike the usual behavior of *G. senegalensis*, *Tarsius bancanus*, and the indriids. The tail is then used to bring the feet down into contact with the support. The momentum of the leap often swivels the body around the support in preparation for an immediate new leap.

Charles-Dominique regards a relatively flat trajectory in the leap, and a horizontal body posture, as facilitating rapid movement through dense undergrowth. In fact, of course, a flat trajectory is a consequence of high speed in movement. Certainly energy costs of leaping would theoretically be high with a flat trajectory, and the matter needs more attention.

As with tarsiers and *Galago senegalensis*, the high frequency of using vertical supports is a natural concomitant of saltatory locomotion near the ground where saplings and tree trunks abound. Apparently in the Gabon forest, however, the presence of "liane curtains" near the ground, as well as in the canopy, further increases the frequency of encountering vertical supports.

Tensile forces in *Galago alleni* are most likely moderate or somewhat high, being engendered primarily by vertical posture and whiplash on landing after leaps. However, small body size may somewhat reduce the biomechanical import of these forces as compared with larger species.

Figure 3.17 shows the polar coordinate plot of the totality of the raw data for this species. *Galago alleni* is somewhat unusual compared with other bushbabies and shows four very distinct rays for ricochetal leaping, undergrowth, vertical supports, and fruit. If much of the fruit is, in fact, on the

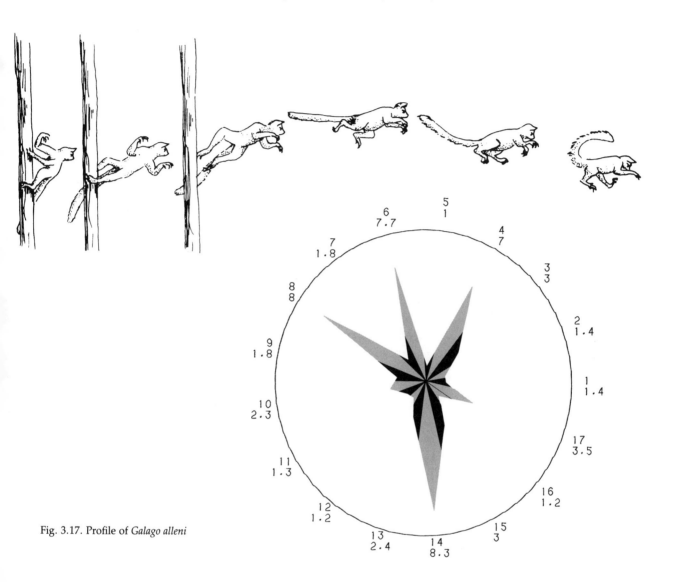

Fig. 3.17. Profile of *Galago alleni*

ground being examined for its contained animal items, rather than consumed as fruit per se, it is possible that the ray for animal items should be larger and that for fruit smaller (see also Redford et al. 1984). However, there are no certain or quantitative estimates of these alternatives.

Galago elegantulus, the needle-clawed bushbaby

Charles-Dominique again provides the fullest account of the locomotion and ecology of this galago from his study at Makoukou (1977). Hladik (1979) and Walker (1979) provide versions of diet and locomotion, respectively. No videotapes or films were available.

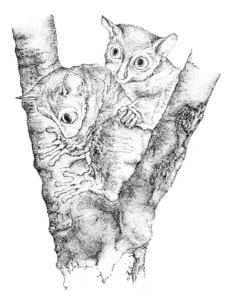

Fig. 3.18. *Galago elegantulus*
(after photograph by Devez)

Despite its small size (about 300 grams), *Galago elegantulus* (figs. 3.18 and 3.19) displays some relationship to *G. crassicaudatus* in its "branch running" habits, and to *Perodicticus* in its use of large and frequently vertical supports during gum feeding. However, some of these similarities are spurious, and comparisons might rather be made with callithricids. As Oates points out (1984), *G. elegantulus*, though a gummivore, feeds on abundant and reliable gum sources. The potto, in contrast, often lives in seasonally unstable environments and must be able to exploit many resources as they are available.

We echo and enlarge this distinction. Specifically, the potto, and even more so, *Galago crassicaudatus*, must be able to exploit gum even if only dry gum is available. This is, presumably, part of the reason for their particular body size, and for some convergences in mandibular and cranial anatomy related to increased robusticity. *G. crassicaudatus* seems to have been the most successful in this respect as it is present even in subtropical regions. Keeled nails have enabled *G. elegantulus* to feed on gum sources unavailable even to the large potto on large tree trunks. Its leaping enables it to move through the canopy without expensive detours, and to utilize gum droplets unavailable to the potto.

Charles-Dominique stresses the frequency of running and leaping in its locomotion, and also falling leaps made between the canopy of one tree and another. In this respect, *Galago crassicaudatus*' locomotion is generally more sedate, although encompassing to some degree all the same behaviors. *G. crassicaudatus* also has keeling on its nails but much less well developed than *G. elegantulus*. In some respects, therefore, *G. crassicaudatus* and *G. elegantulus* are linked, in that they are gummivorous galagos, but the particular foraging strategy of the former links the greater bushbaby more closely with the potto.

Charles-Dominique's assessments for the use of supports under 1 centimeter must then be underestimated if *Galago elegantulus* does indeed frequently use foliage as a "soft" target for its falling leaps. In detail, the running locomotion of *G. elegantulus* as described by Charles-Dominique seems to be rather potto-like in that the limbs are used in abducted positions. Charles-Dominique says that "rapid locomotion is essentially achieved by a series of short leaps." This may indicate that *G. elegantulus*' running is actually more like scurrying, as in *G. demodovii*, and it may grade into leaping as speed increases because of a limitation in stride length. Our figure for scurrying may be an underestimate and that for slow quadrupedalism, an overestimate.

Charles-Dominique calls *Galago elegantulus* the "most effective leaping form," a description which is difficult to see in comparison with *G. alleni*.

In describing the typical leap of *Galago elegantulus*, Charles-Dominique notes that the trajectory is high and the body "held erect throughout." Unlike the long leaps of *G. senegalensis*, however, the hindlimbs appear to trail and the body is not curled up in mid-flight. Landing is onto the forelimb as

Fig. 3.19. *Galago elegantulus* (after Devez)

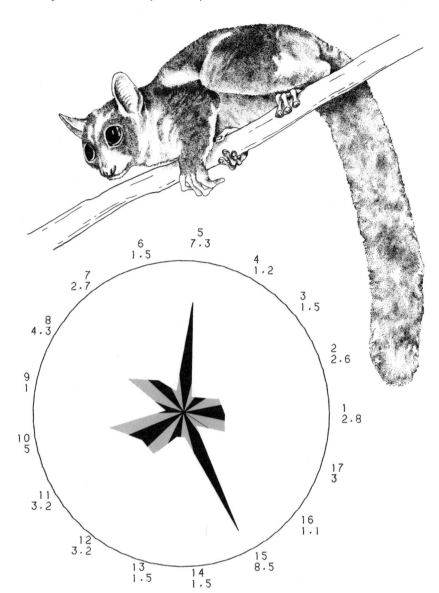

Fig. 3.20. Profile of *Galago elegantulus*

in *G. crassicaudatus*, but the latter retracts its hindlimbs in flight, only extending them before landing, which *G. elegantulus* apparently does not do.

Tensile forces in *G. elegantulus* might be relatively high for such a small animal, being generated by vertical suspensory postures and whiplash of landing branches after falls in leaping.

Figure 3.20 shows the polar coordinate plot of the totality of the raw data for this species. The longest rays point to canopy, and gums and nectar. There are somewhat lesser rays pointing toward larger and vertical supports, toward running and falling leaps, and toward animal items in the diet.

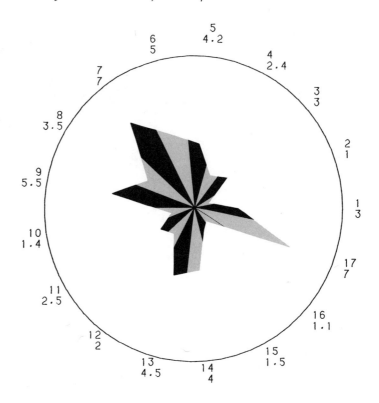

Fig. 3.21. Profile of *Galago zanzibaricus*

Galago zanzibaricus, the Zanzibar galago

Galago zanzibaricus, originally included in *G. senegalensis*, is now recognized as distinct at the species level. It has been studied by Nash (1983) and by Harcourt (personal communication) near Gedi in Kenya. Notes are also available in Kingdon (1971). No videotape or film was available.

Nash's observations tend to confirm Kingdon's reports that *Galago zanzibaricus* deviates from *G. senegalensis* in a rather *G. demidovii*-like direction. Its locomotion involves much leaping, but tends toward scurrying. It occupies the forest understory, unlike the Gabonese *G. demidovii*, an inhabitant of the canopy. It appears to use foliage much more frequently than *G. senegalensis*, and it also uses vertical supports a little more frequently than the lesser bushbaby. *G. zanzibaricus* appears more similar to the local *G. crassicaudatus* variant, *G. garnettii*, in its diet than is the case with *G. senegalensis* and *G. crassicaudatus* in Southern Africa. Both of the former pair of species are more frugivorous than the southern pair.

Nash notes that head-down clinging posture, striking but infrequent in *Galago senegalensis*, is fully 18 percent of postural observations. We do not have sufficient data on locomotion to discuss fully the dietary preferences, habitat utilizations, and locomotor activities in *G. zanzibaricus*.

Figure 3.21 shows the polar coordinate plot of the totality of the raw data for this species. The longest rays point toward animal dietary items, and horizontal and small supports; lesser rays toward scurrying and fruit-eating; and minor rays toward falling, crouching, and ricochetal leaping.

Fig. 3.22. *Galago senegalensis*
(redrawn after Estey)

Galago senegalensis, the lesser bushbaby

Inadequate information prevents us from utilizing a division of *Galago se-negalensis* into three species (*G. gallarum*, *G. moholi*, and *G. senegalensis*) as some taxonomists prefer.

The locomotor behavior of *Galago senegalensis* (figs. 3.22 and 3.23) was studied with the animal in captivity and in the field by Crompton, and other observations have been made by Bearder (1974) and Harcourt (1980). Crompton took videotape of the lesser bushbaby in captivity and in the field.

Galago senegalensis is largely insectivorous, but may rely very heavily on gums of *Acacia* in the winter months. Its locomotion is rather similar to that of *G. zanzibaricus*, but without the frequent scurrying of the latter species. It seems to use a wider variety of supports than does *G. zanzibaricus*, but moves rather more often lower down, at least in this study. Crompton (1980, 1984) regards the saltatory locomotion of *G. senegalensis* as an adaptation to movement in the lower treetrunk and ground zone, allowing rapid and safe exploration for scarce arthropods and efficient utilization of the more reliable gum sites of tree and sapling trunks during dry periods in an intensely seasonal environment.

Fig. 3.23. *Galago senegalensis* (after a photograph by Roots)

Not surprisingly our profile for *Galago senegalensis* shows similarities to the more unspecialized of the tarsiers, although differing from them in its reasonably common scurrying and quadrupedal running and less frequent use of vertical supports, as it differs from *Tarsius* species in its partly gum-mivorous diet. There are also weaker resemblances to the more specialized *G. alleni*, all of which move in the same low arboreal zone, largely by salta-tion. Running in these species does not grade into leaping, as it does to various degrees in *G. elegantulus*, *G. crassicaudatus*, *G. demidovii*, and some cheirogaleines. The occasions on which running plays a similar role to leap-ing could be expected to be more common in *G. senegalensis* than in the Tarsiidae at least.

Leaping in *Galago senegalensis* can be crudely classed in three types. First, there are short leaps in which the body is held in a horizontal position and the tail relatively inactive, and in which the forelimbs make the initial con-tact and absorb most of the force of landing. Second are hopping leaps. These occur between near-vertical supports or often as an intermediate ricochetal-like extension of an earlier, usually crouching, leap. In hopping leaps there is no forelimb involvement on landing, and there may be little on take-off. This kind of leap occurs in the indriids. The third type involves a crouching preparation, full retraction of the hindlimbs and forelimbs dur-ing flight so that the body assumes a curled up vertical posture, and tail activity rotating the body. A further rotation of the body using a tail-flick (just as in Niemitz' 1979 and 1984 reports of *Tarsius bancanus* leaping) brings the feet forward to make the landing with the legs extended in front of the body.

Galago senegalensis thus utilizes various styles of leaping, while some other species use one style exclusively. The biomechanical and behavioral significance of "leaping style" will be the subject of a further paper.

The walking motion of *Galago senegalensis*, in contrast, is awkward and infrequent. *G. senegalensis* climbs slowly, with hindlimb propulsion predom-inating, and occasionally uses a froglike "shinning" (described by Niemitz [1979, 1984] for *Tarsius bancanus*). There is apparently no regularly used gait pattern in *G. senegalensis* climbing, as there is with the large lorisines. Climbing is, however, a reasonably common and important part of *G. sene-galensis* locomotion.

Galago senegalensis, like *G. demidovii* and *Microcebus*, includes as part of its less common (under 5 percent) locomotor behaviors, cantilevering, the ex-tension of the body away from the vertical like a spring from the stable base of the feet. This is likely to produce high bending stresses in the ankle and foot regions, and high tensile stresses in the longer segments of the lower leg and foot. It is particularly associated with capturing insect prey. At about the same frequency, *G. senegalensis* descends vertical or highly angled supports in inverted positions, with navicular-calcaneal rotation to "re-verse" the feet. This behavior is partly connected with access to gum sites on tree and sapling trunks, and partly related (as with the froglike climbing

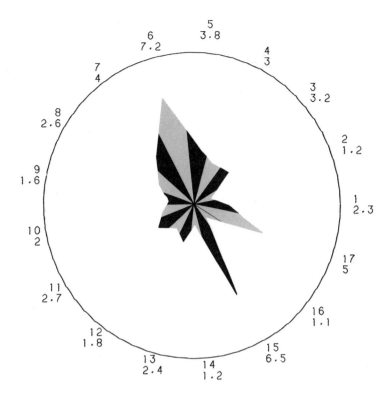

Fig. 3.24. Profile of *Galago senegalensis*

and sliding down tree trunks in *Tarsius bancanus* [Niemitz 1979, 1984]), to movement to and from look-out points in foraging for prey on the ground.

An infrequent but striking posture, and one which may be of relatively high importance, is head-down clinging, which occurred in a third of observations of gum feeding. Head-down clinging seems more common in *Galago zanzibaricus*, and less common in *G. crassicaudatus*, so its connection with gum-feeding may not be significant. It is likely to produce tensile stresses in limbs (though not necessarily, of course, within limb bones).

The polar coordinate plot for this species is shown in figure 3.24. It shows longest rays toward gums and nectar, and animal dietary items, and somewhat lesser rays toward undergrowth and scurrying. Most of the leaping variables are also well represented.

Galago demidovii, Demidoff's bushbaby

Galago demidovii (fig. 3.25) has been studied in the field by Charles-Dominique at Makoukou, Gabon (1979), and further notes were made by Jewell and Oates (1969) in Nigeria and by Kingdon in Kenya (1971). Crompton (1980) observed the animal in captivity and Hladik (1979) reviewed its diet. Video-recordings of *G. demidovii* were taken by Crompton.

According to Charles-Dominique, on whose account of the Makoukou population we principally rely, *Galago demidovii* in tropical rainforest is pre-

Fig. 3.25. *Galago demidovii*
(after a photograph by Devez)

dominantly a denizen of the high canopy. Here it prefers to inhabit liane curtains, which provide an abundance of small, vertical supports. Elsewhere it has been reported to live in the undergrowth, where it selects tangled vegetation. Crompton's captive specimens were moving on the cage floor in 10 percent of observations, but whether or not this reflects the existence of ground activity in some populations of freeranging *G. demidovii* cannot be determined. *Galago demidovii* exhibits a strong preference for small supports, and appears to prefer vertical or oblique supports to horizontal ones, if availability permits.

There is general agreement between Charles-Dominique's field study and Crompton's observation of captive animals. However, Walker's data (1979) show striking differences to these studies. Most notably, Walker's animals included hopping in their locomotor repertoire, while the other animals were not seen to hop. It now seems likely that Walker's animals were not *G. demidovii*, but a sister species, *G. thomasii*.

Galago demidovii's diet is primarily insectivorous, fruits and gums making up the remainder. It may compete with *Arctocebus* in foliage and liane tangles in Makoukou, since there is a great deal of niche overlap in diet and support preferences. In its locomotion there is little overlap with *Arctocebus*, however, as it is markedly saltatorial. Leaping is not quite as frequent as in adult *G. senegalensis* (at about 40 percent) in both studies undertaken in captivity. Those two studies, particularly Crompton's, found running quite common. Charles-Dominique also stresses the adaptation of *G. demidovii* for running as well as leaping, and regards its extreme tarsal elongation as an adaptation for both.

We have chosen to characterize the usual quadrupedal movement pattern of *Galago demidovii* as scurrying. It typically consists of rapid but brief movement sequences, which may change smoothly and without interruption

into very short leaps, and back to quadrupedalism. When a high-angled support continues on from a horizontal support, the same type of scurrying appears to be employed for both. There is a marked contrast with typical *G. senegalensis* locomotion, in which locomotion changes from walking to climbing to running and so on. There is some similarity with *G. senegalensis*, on the other hand, because *G. senegalensis* does include a motion that may be classified as scurrying. Scurrying in *G. demidovii* naturally grades into running leaping.

Leaping in *Galago demidovii* has been described by Charles-Dominique, and Crompton's studies for the most part confirm his description. The body is held in a horizontal posture, with the limbs outstretched or hanging down. The forelimbs seem to land first. The tail is used to rotate the body about its long axis, or to make corrections of balance on landing.

Charles-Dominique stresses the flat trajectory of the leap as an adaptation to densely packed supports in its natural habitat of liane curtains or under-growth tangles. The precise curvature of a trajectory, however, is based upon the speed and distance of the leap. Its relationship with support density and orientation must be complex, and will require more attention.

Cantilevering behavior was observed in Crompton's study of *Galago demidovii* at frequencies similar to those obtaining in *G. senegalensis*. Tensile forces in *G. demidovii* are not likely otherwise to be very high, and would be induced mainly by branch whiplash during leaping and suspensory behavior.

The polar coordinate plot for this species is shown in figure 3.26. It is a "flying bird-shaped" envelope with the "wings" pointing toward animal dietary items and small supports, the "beak" toward the canopy, and the "tail" toward scurrying. Several of the leaping variables are well represented, as are horizontal and vertical supports.

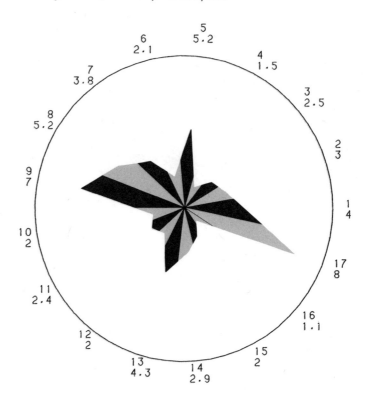

Fig. 3.26. Profile of *Galago demidovii*

Tarsiidae

Tarsius bancanus, the western tarsier

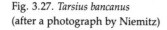

Fig. 3.27. *Tarsius bancanus*
(after a photograph by Niemitz)

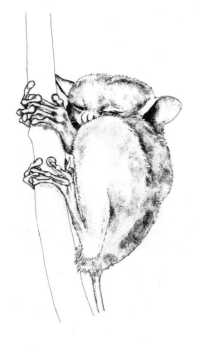

Tarsius bancanus (fig. 3.27) has been studied extensively in semi-natural captive conditions by Niemitz (e.g., 1979, 1983, 1984a, 1984b) in Sarawak, largely at Semongok with some observations on freeranging specimens. Notes were also made by Fogden (1974). A systematic study of freeranging specimens is now being carried out by Crompton at Sepilok in Sabah. Videotape of wild-born specimens was made by Crompton.

Tarsius bancanus is entirely carnivorous and insectivorous, as far as is known. It is described by Niemitz as moving almost exclusively by leaping between vertical supports, selecting those of about 3 to 4 centimeters in diameter. Although Fogden reported sighting *T. bancanus* commonly above 3 meters and even as high as 8 meters, Niemitz believes they spend most of their time below one meter and that they rarely go above 3 meters except to sleep. At present, then, the species seems to be largely restricted to the undergrowth and the present radio-tracking study will provide a firm answer to this question. Here we have adopted a conservative figure for use of the undergrowth.

Climbing behavior is present, but not common, and consists partly of froglike leaps up vertical supports, shinning up and sliding down rather than climbing in the usual sense. Forelimb involvement is present. Walking is rare but occurs when *Tarsius* is on the ground, presumably in a context

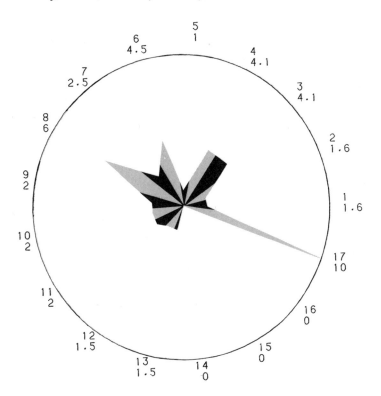

Fig. 3.28. Profile of *Tarsius bancanus*

similar to that which induces *Galago senegalensis* to walk on the ground: ex-amination of the forest floor for prey items. *T. bancanus* usually returns to the tree trunk immediately with captured prey and does not generally cross the ground by hopping as does *G. senegalensis*. In trees, a small amount of scurrying may occur. But in general, it seems that *T. bancanus'* locomotion and habitat use are highly uniform.

It seems to prefer dense forest where gaps are small between supports (most leaps are 1.5 meters or less), and it is found in greater numbers in secondary than in primary forest. In regenerating forest, vertical supports are more abundant near the ground. Generally, small supports predomi-nate, but Niemitz has shown that 3 to 4 centimeter supports are differen-tially selected.

The leaping and quadrupedal locomotion of *Tarsius bancanus* has been thoroughly described by Niemitz (1983). Its crouching leaps closely re-semble those of *Galago senegalensis*, with body upright; but from Niemitz' illustrations, it does not appear that the limbs are retracted as much as in the lesser bushbaby. Niemitz does not mention how many leaps are ricoch-etal, involving repeated landings and take-offs. Tensile forces in *T. bancanus'* locomotion are probably generated by whiplash of branches during leaping, and could be quite high and frequent but not last long. Overall, *T. bancanus* must be one of the most highly specialized of primates. The polar coordi-nate plot for this species is shown in figure 3.28. This very distinctive plot shows four isolated rays toward animal dietary items, vertical supports, undergrowth, and crouching and ricochetal leaping.

Crompton's interim findings from a radio-tracking study of *Tarsius bancanus* were published during a late stage of the production of this book (Crompton and Andau 1986). On the whole, but with some reservations, they confirm the general character of the summary and plot provided here on the basis of Niemitz' earlier work. We have decided, therefore, not to modify the summary, plot, or attributions presented above, but will provide the new data here for reference. A detailed quantitative discussion of locomotion, habitat use, and diet is now available in Crompton and Andau (1986); ranging and social behavior are discussed in Crompton and Andau (1987).

According to Crompton and Andau's most recent studies, *Tarsius bancanus* is indeed primarily a creature of the lowest parts of the undergrowth, although it may be sighted at 10 meters or more when resting or when its route requires it. The affinity for verticals and supports of from 2 to 4 centimeters as recorded by Niemitz is confirmed. Locomotion is predominantly by crouching and ricochetal leaping at just above ground level. Climbing is common and occurs primarily between leaps, when the height of vertical supports changes, or when the animal is examining the ground for prey.

Prey, made up largely of beetles, cockroaches, crickets, grasshoppers, and some moths (with some crabs and frogs taken opportunistically), are captured mainly on the ground. However, the cantilever movement noted for some lorisids was observed in several cases when tarsiers were taking moths from supports above ground level. Tarsiers leap to the ground to examine and seize potential prey, but may walk clumsily on the ground in "detailed foraging." Some individual tarsiers do hop on the ground, but not for any great distance; it is not a common activity.

In general, Crompton and Andau found that tarsier behavior, although relatively specialized, is more labile than appears from Niemitz' report on captive specimens. Leaping formed 61 percent of locomotion. This is actually less than the MacKinnons' report for *Tarsius spectrum* (1980), although their figure is probably too high. Our plot, based on Niemitz' description of captive animals, is therefore an overestimate. Studies of captives do regularly seem to exaggerate figures in this way. Crompton (1980) found that 70.7 percent of the locomotion of captive *Galago senegalensis* was leaping, versus 53 percent in his study of freeranging individuals. Considerable caution must therefore be taken in interpreting the results of studies of locomotion in captive animals.

Tarsius spectrum, the spectral tarsier

The spectral tarsier (figs. 3.29 and 3.30) has been studied in the field by MacKinnon and MacKinnon (1980) at Tangkoko-Batuangas, Sulawesi. Additional notes were made by Niemitz in Northern and Central Sulawesi (1984b). No videotapes or film records were available.

The MacKinnons' report indicates that in general *Tarsius spectrum* is considerably less specialized than *T. bancanus*, and this makes its behavior somewhat resemble that of *Galago senegalensis*, as Niemitz notes. Although when traveling, *T. spectrum* chose the same small, and mostly vertical, support size as *T. bancanus*, in other activities larger supports and usually oblique and horizontal ones were chosen instead. Though most activity occurs under 3 meters, Niemitz made observations on *T. spectrum* as high as 20 meters and noted a strong association between height differences and support usage differences because of differences in habitat structure. The diet of *T. spectrum*, however, still seems largely or exclusively carnivorous or insectivorous.

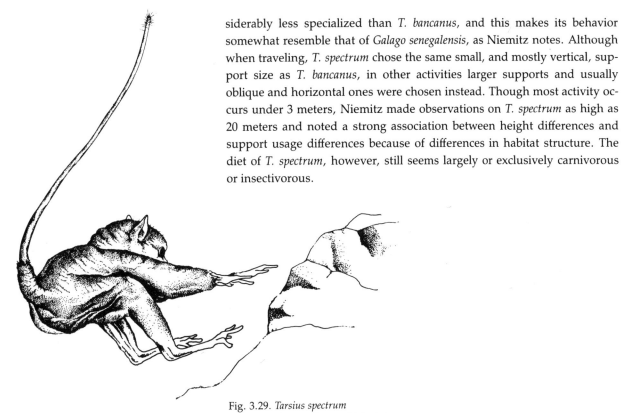

Fig. 3.29. *Tarsius spectrum*
(redrawn after Walker and Napier)

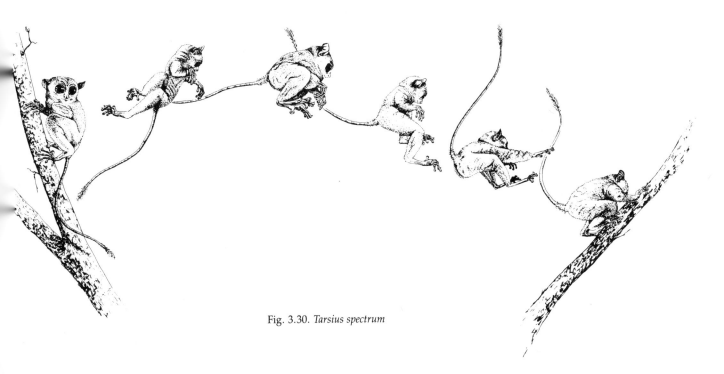

Fig. 3.30. *Tarsius spectrum*

The MacKinnons gave figures for non-saltatory locomotion (without stating sample size), but their categories are nonstandard, and we have made rough estimations from them. It seems that scurrying behavior and perhaps running leaping may be more common, and climbing considerably more common, in *Tarsius spectrum* than in *T. bancanus*. The MacKinnons describe "loris-like clambering quadrumanually" in this species "through branch or liane thickets." They do not mention walking at all. Leaping accounts for 63 percent of locomotion, a figure much more like that in *Galago senegalensis* (53 percent) than that implied by Niemitz' report of *T. bancanus*, and considerably less than the high figure (70.7 percent) obtained for captive *G. senegalensis* in Crompton's 1980 study. We do not have any descriptions of the style of leaping in *T. spectrum*.

Tensile forces may again be quite high, from whiplash in leaping, and also from the "loris-like clambering." In general, then, *Tarsius spectrum* seems to be a much less specialized tarsier than *T. bancanus*, with many similarities to *Galago senegalensis*. This cannot be reflected adequately in our plot (fig. 3.31), as locomotor data are too scanty. Like that for the western tarsier, this plot is very distinctive. There are four isolated rays toward animal dietary items, vertical supports, undergrowth, and crouching and ricochetal leaping.

Fig. 3.31. Profile of *Tarsius spectrum*

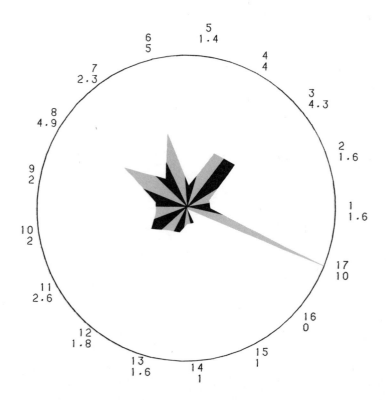

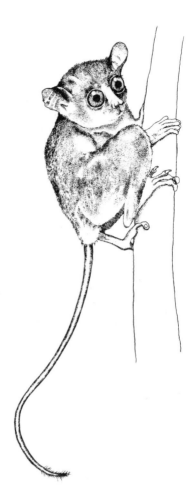

Tarsius syrichta, the Philippines tarsier

At present, we have only the limited observations of Sprankel (1965) on captive *Tarsius syrichta* to rely on, and virtually no knowledge of the behavior of wild *T. syrichta* beyond some unsystematic observations also reviewed by Sprankel. A film was taken at the Zoological Society of London some years ago but illustrates only the leaping style.

We have tried to estimate the main differences in the behaviors of *Tarsius syrichta* and *T. bancanus* from Sprankel's remarks, but our locomotor profile must be, at best, tentative. Wild *T. syrichta* (fig. 3.32) seem to prefer the regenerating secondary forests and plantations. They seem to move more often on the ground by scurrying as well as running and hopping. If anything, reports available indicate that they are even more restricted to undergrowth than is *T. bancanus*, moving in open as well as dense areas. If Sprankel's observations of captive animals also apply to the field situation, then *T. syrichta* might use horizontal supports much more than *T. bancanus*, and rather larger branches than either *T. bancanus* or *T. spectrum*. They may not be as exclusively carnivorous and insectivorous, since Sprankel reports feeding bananas to his captive *T. syrichta*. The leap of *T. syrichta* seems very similar to that of *T. bancanus*, with hindlimbs landing first and the body being held vertical during the flight phase. However, data on *T. syrichta* are so inadequate that these conclusions must be very tentative.

The polar coordinate plot for this species is shown in figure 3.33. There are two very long isolated rays toward animal dietary items and undergrowth. Crouching and ricochetal leaping are somewhat less emphasized. There is a short ray toward vertical supports.

Fig. 3.32. *Tarsius syrichta* (after a photograph by Wright)

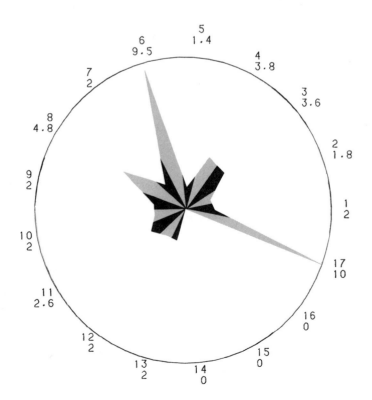

Fig. 3.33. Profile of *Tarsius syrichta*

Fig. 3.34. *Microcebus murinus*
(after a photograph by Dean), showing
tensile loading.

Cheirogaleinae

Microcebus murinus, the lesser mouse lemur

Martin (1972) has studied the mouse lemur (figs. 3.34 and 3.35) in the field at Madena in the Malagasy Republic. Reviews of locomotion are available in Walker (1979) and Tattersall (1982). The latter discusses diet and ecology, and Hladik (1979) also reviews diet. Crompton (1980) has observed captive *Microcebus*, made a quantitative summary of their locomotor behavior, and made videotape records.

Compared with the larger *Cheirogaleus medius*, *Microcebus murinus* is much more agile. Appropriate to its very small size, its diet is much more insectivorous than that of *C. medius*, although, according to Hladik, a few more fruit than arthropods are taken. Its locomotion is generally rather similar to that of *Galago demidovii*, being largely short scurrying runs, but with fewer intercalated leaps than in *G. demidovii*. At high speeds the scurrying may change into a bounding gait, rather than a leap, as tends to happen in *G. demidovii*. The body is not held close to the substrate as in *C. medius*, nor is the tail used as actively as a balancing organ as in *G. demidovii*. *Microcebus murinus*, like *G. demidovii* are capable of continuing their scurrying runs up vertical supports.

Leaping is the next most frequent type of locomotion. Apart from those running and falling leaps, leaps are prefaced by a preparatory crouch. *Microcebus murinus* can apparently take off either with the body facing the support or transverse to the support, but always the head looks toward the target. The trajectory is high, the body is held horizontally, the limbs are stretched out, and the tail serves to rotate the body into its horizontal position. Only forelimb-first landing has been observed by Crompton, although some leaps were over 1.5 meters. Height may be gained in leaps of a meter or less; beyond that the animal tends to lose height. Walker reports froglike leaps on the ground, which may be similar to our bounding quadrupedal gait. Climbing is less common but quite agile, and involves frequent bridging and cantilevering, which must place high tensile loads on the body and limbs. *M. murinus* can climb along underneath a branch or spiral around it, but more frequently these animals move on top.

In our study all four orientations of support—vertical, steeply angled, gently sloped, and horizontal—were commonly used, although horizontals were a little more commonly selected than the others. The animals used a wide variety of supports in our studies but in the wild are reported to use supports under 1 centimeter most often. Therefore, with caution, we have plotted them so.

Microcebus murinus in the wild is reported by Martin as inhabiting the forest fringe habitat, in dense tangles of foliage. These tangles, however, were at undergrowth level in secondary forest, but in primary forest were

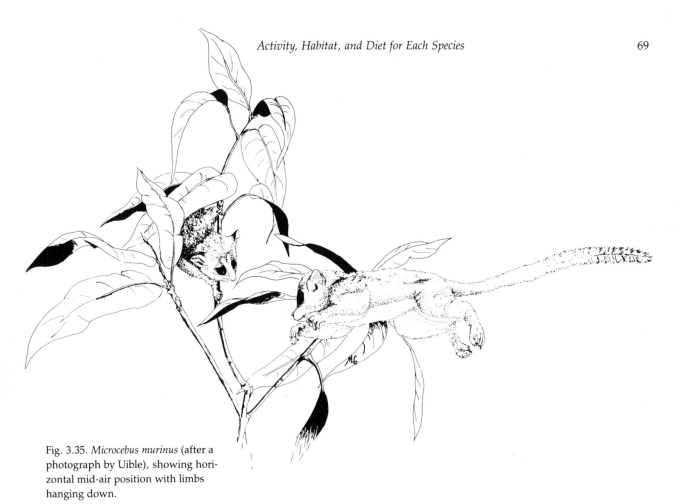

Fig. 3.35. *Microcebus murinus* (after a photograph by Uible), showing horizontal mid-air position with limbs hanging down.

in the canopy at over 30 meters. The parallels with *Galago demidovii* are quite marked and, of course, Charles-Dominique and Martin (1970) have themselves noted the general similarity of the two species, and their status as a possible model for the ancestral stock of primates of modern aspect. But it is *Microcebus murinus* rather than *G. demidovii* whose plasticity and variety of locomotor behavior strikes us as a ready basis on which to build very many of the prosimian locomotor adaptations (Crompton, in preparation). Suspensory postures are quite common whether head-up or head-down, and *M. murinus* can sustain itself on supports of over 30 centimeters in diameter using cracks in the bark.

The polar coordinate plot for this species is shown in figure 3.36. The envelope for this species is also like a "flying bird." The "wings" point toward animal dietary items and small supports, the very large "tail" toward scurrying and fruit items, and the smaller "beak" toward the canopy. Various forms of leaping are also represented, especially crouching leaping.

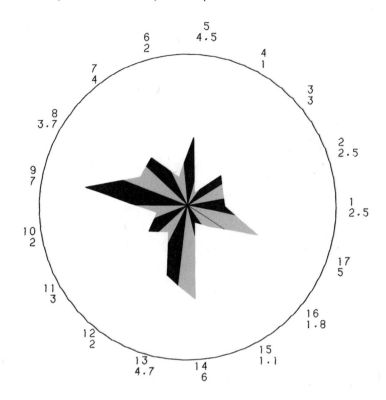

Fig. 3.36. Profile of *Microcebus murinus*

Cheirogaleus medius, the fat-tailed dwarf lemur

We do not have enough data to make separate profiles for *Cheirogaleus medius* and *C. major* (fig. 3.37). Petter et al. (1977) are quoted by Tattersall (1982) in a brief review of both species, and Walker (1979) also reviews their locomotion. According to Tattersall, however, the two versions gave opposite descriptions of the differences between them. We therefore concentrate here on descriptions of *C. medius* since a short film by Petter was available to us. The profile is tentative, based upon estimation rather than measurement. We rely on Hladik's (1979) report of the diet of *C. medius*.

Cheirogaleus medius is reported to live in "the lowest three to five meters of the forest" (Walker 1979), but Martin (1972) reports that they were rarely found below three meters. It seems that they prefer supports of large diameter, and sloping or horizontal rather than vertical. Locomotion is primarily scurrying, a little less commonly walking in a diagonal gait, and considerably less often climbing awkwardly on small supports, but down trunks quite quickly. The body is held very close to the branch and the tail

Fig. 3.37. *Cheirogaleus medius* (after a photograph by Visser)

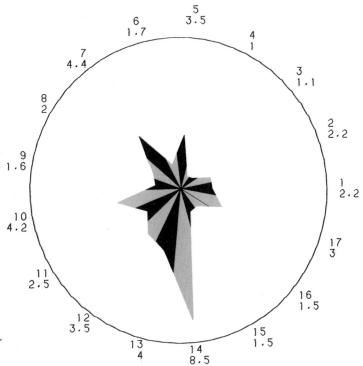

Fig. 3.38. Profile of *Cheirogaleus medius/major*

is held out flat. *C. medius'* balance on small supports, when the tail is held out flat, seems rather poor. The stratum utilized, according to Martin (1972), is linked to the strong substrate preference for large horizontal supports.

Their leaping seems predominantly short running or falling leaps. In falling leaps the body is horizontal with the limbs held out laterally so that the animal "glides" a little. In the very few leaps observed, the tail is inactive and the forelimbs land first. The diet of *Cheirogaleus medius* is largely frugivorous but includes nectar and some insects. *C. medius* have been reported to feed on homopteran secretions.

The polar coordinate plot for this species is shown in figure 3.38. A single, very large ray points toward fruit. Smaller rays distinguish animal items and running leaping, canopy, horizontal supports, and large supports. Scurrying, slow climbing, and slow quadrupedalism are also all represented to some degree in this plot.

Microcebus coquereli, Coquerel's mouse lemur

Coquerel's mouse lemur has been studied in the field by Petter et al. (1971) and by Pagés (1978) at Morondava in the Malagasy Republic. Walker (1979), Hladik (1979), and Tattersall (1982) review its behavior. No video or film records were available to us.

Microcebus coquereli is much larger than *M. murinus*, but a little lighter than

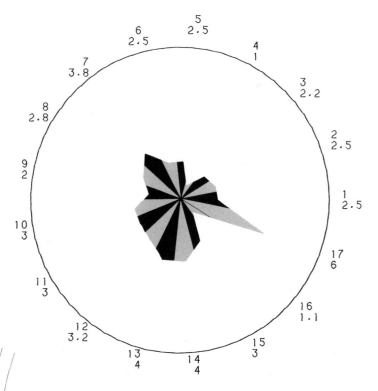

Fig. 3.39. Profile of *Microcebus coquereli*

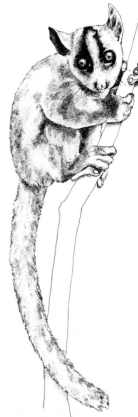

Fig. 3.40. *Phaner furcifer*
(after a photograph by Petter)

Cheirogaleus medius. Its diet is seasonally variable. In wet seasons it may feed on fruit, flowers, insects, and small vertebrates, including *M. murinus*; in the dry season it becomes dependent on the secretions of homopteran larvae. It moves primarily in the lower six meters of the forest, mainly by scurrying on horizontal supports, but often also up and down verticals.

Suspensory postures are reasonably common, but less common, perhaps, than in *Phaner*. It is likely to be subjected to fewer tensile forces than is *Phaner* or *Microcebus*. Lack of any quantitative data or film record renders our profile tentative.

The polar coordinate plot for this species is shown in figure 3.39. It has relatively short rays for most variables, with a fairly small envelope. Animal dietary items are distinguished at an intermediate level.

Phaner furcifer, the fork-marked dwarf lemur

Phaner (fig. 3.40) has been studied in the field by Petter, Schilling, and Pariente (1971, 1975) at Analabe in the Malagasy Republic, and its behavior is reviewed by Walker (1979), Hladik (1979), and Tattersall (1982). No video or film records were available.

The locomotion of *Phaner* seems to be similar to that of *Microcebus coquereli*; however, it is a little heavier and feeds largely on gums and saps. Its primary mode of locomotion is by scurrying, interspersed by running leaps

Fig. 3.41. Profile of *Phaner furcifer*

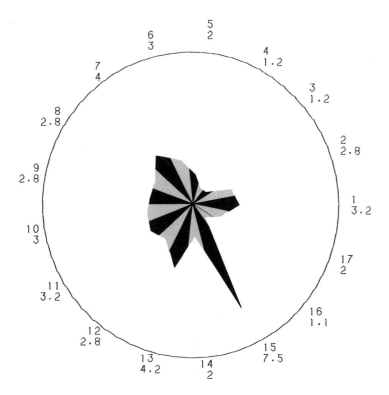

and falling leaps between terminal branches of trees. Horizontal displacements of four to five meters are recorded in falling leaps. Considerable loss of height may occur, giving the leaps total lengths of ten meters or so.

Its locomotion, by all accounts, is faster than that of *Cheirogaleus medius*, despite its greater size. Slow quadrupedalism may be a little less common, but climbing somewhat more common. Keeled nails (like those of *Galago elegantulus*) give *Phaner* access to large branches of tree trunks while searching for sap and gum sites. However, as it prefers horizontal supports, its vertical stratum of the forest depends upon the location of most horizontal branches in the particular local forest type in which it is observed. In the study of Petter et al., it was most often found at about three to four meters above the ground, although it has been observed both in the canopy and upon the ground.

Suspensory postures, most often head-down clinging while feeding on vertical supports, seem more common than in *M. coquereli*. As with many other cheirogaleines and galagines, both forelimb and hindlimb suspension were observed. Tensile forces may be quite common because of the suspensory postures and frequent falling leaps onto foliage, with consequent whiplash.

The polar coordinate plot for this species is shown in figure 3.41. This plot, too, has a rather small envelope, with the dietary items gums and nectar being especially distinguished.

Daubentoniidae

Daubentonia madagascariensis, the aye-aye

Daubentonia (figs. 3.42 and 3.43) has been studied in the field by Petter and Peyriéras (1970a) at Mahombo in the Malagasy Republic, and reviews are available in Hladik (1979), Walker (1979), and Tattersall (1982). Brief film records were available.

Descriptions of *Daubentonia* locomotion, although unquantified, are adequate for producing an acceptable profile. Locomotion seems to be composed largely of slow quadrupedal climbing and walking. Clawed digits enable similar locomotion on supports of varying orientation, but the elongated fingers necessitate dorsiflexion of the wrists and support on palmar pads when walking on horizontal substrates. This produces an awkward gait with an exaggerated stride length but slow maximum speed. As usual with lemurs, the ipsilateral hindfoot and forefoot meet in walking. Froglike leaps may be intercalated into walking or running, with four limbs landing together. This seems also to be similar to the way in which some squirrels land on all four limbs on jumping to the ground. Longer leaps are also reported by Walker, but these are more hesitant than in most lemurs. They may be used to cross between terminal branches of neighboring trees. Bridging behavior is also reported by Petter and Peyriéras in this situation.

Little is known about stratum preference. *Daubentonia* are known, however, to come to the ground quite frequently. Little is known either about the relationship between habitat structure and locomotion. The diet of fruits (apparently often coconuts at Mahombo) and grubs taken from holes in branches would indicate some preference for large supports, probably more often horizontal than vertical.

Suspensory locomotion has also been reported by Walker, consisting of climbing along or "walking" underneath large diameter supports, and hindlimb suspension seems a common posture in which to eat fruit. These, and bridging behavior, would be a major source of tensile forces, along with vertical climbing.

The polar coordinate plot for this species is shown in figure 3.44. It is rather distinctive, being shaped like a clover leaf with a stem. The three "leaflets" point toward (a) animal items, (b) the combination of canopy, undergrowth, and horizontal and vertical supports, and (c) the combination of large supports, climbing, and slow quadrupedalism. The "stalk" indicates the fruit in the diet.

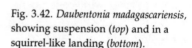

Fig. 3.42. *Daubentonia madagascariensis*, showing suspension (*top*) and in a squirrel-like landing (*bottom*).

Fig. 3.43. *Daubentonia*

Fig. 3.44. Profile of *Daubentonia*

Indriidae

Indri indri, the indri or babakoto

The behavior of *Indri* has been reported by Petter and Peyriéras (1974), and in greater depth by Pollock (1975, 1977) from a field study at Anamalazoatra in the Malagasy Republic, and reviewed by Walker (1979), Hladik (1979), and Tattersall (1982). A short section of film was available.

Pollock's research confirms that the locomotion of *Indri* is indeed highly specialized. Vertical and steeply angled supports are favored over horizontal. *Indri* move primarily by *ricochetal* leaping, although climbing down tree trunks and brief quadrupedal movements in the periphery of the trees are also noted by Walker. While Walker describes *Indri* as hopping when on the ground, Pollock rather emphasizes its avoidance of the ground. This is in contradistinction to the situation in *Propithecus verreauxi*. Instead, says Pollock, *Indri* utilize and leap between any available angled or vertical large supports, and do not move on the ground itself if at all possible.

Body postures are reported as commonly clinging to vertical supports

Fig. 3.45. *Indri indri* (after a photograph by Attenborough) showing vertical clinging.

Fig. 3.46. *Indri indri* leaping.

with strongly flexed legs and with arms outstretched and abducted (figs. 3.45 and 3.46). This seems to be reminiscent of the posture of a repairman climbing a telegraph pole, or a lumberjack aided by a climbing loop on a treetrunk. This posture creates a force component pressing the feet against the substrate and resisting falling. It also creates tensile components in the forelimbs. Sitting postures, quite often in tree forks with all four limbs in support, also often utilize forelimb positions in which they must be bearing some tension. These postures are probably more common than has been reported.

As sometimes with *Tarsius bancanus*, *Indri* climb tree trunks with froglike thrusts of the hindlimbs together. *Indri* usually descend trunks by backward quadrumanual climbing, thus producing marked tensile forces within the forelimbs.

Indri seem to move just below, rather than in, the canopy, and as Pollock suggests, their locomotion gives them access to emergents and to discontinuous canopy. They are not, however, necessarily at any advantage over true canopy-dwellers (such as *Lemur fulvus*) in their access to continuous canopy, especially as they more often lose than gain height on leaps. *Indri* come to ground level every day to eat newly exposed earth, and are individually variable in height preference.

Leaping is most commonly ricochetal, as we have observed. In a typical ricochetal leap sequence, comprised of from two to eight leaps according to Pollock, the arms first relax, allowing the upper body to fall away from the support before the flexed hindlimbs thrust off. (This indicates, incidentally, yet another mode in which the forelimbs are bearing tensile forces as suggested by Oxnard 1983). The hindlimbs are flexed again, shortly after take-off and the arms held at shoulder height or above. The body is usually held in a near-vertical position during the leap. The hindlimbs extend shortly before landing thus absorbing shock, but sometimes both pairs of limbs simultaneously, or the forelimbs alone, make the initial contact. Flexion of the legs prepares them for an immediate second take-off, in which only one leg may be giving the main thrust, or both, depending upon support and body orientation. In long leaps the extended arms may stretch the lateral body skin so that it can act somewhat as a flying membrane; with this position is assumed a more horizontal body posture. The leaps generally lose height and are not parabolic in trajectory (further suggesting aerodynamic modification, as indicated by Oxnard 1983).

Suspensory postures, even forelimb suspension, have been noted in feeding, although they do not seem by any means as common as in *Propithecus verreauxi*. Tensile forces on the forelimb, in particular, will be high to very high (for a prosimian) in *Indri*, because of the various body postures outlined above, in vertical clinging, in suspensory feeding positions, in backwards downward climbing, and in some of the landing mechanisms after leaping, given the momentum of the body in ricochetal leaping at this body weight (discussed in Oxnard 1983).

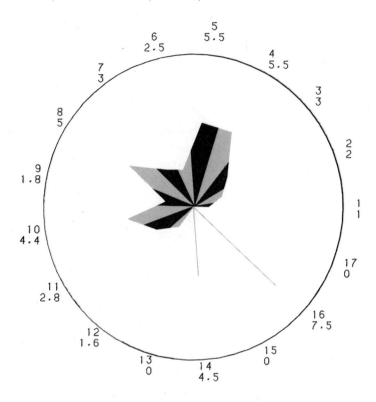

Fig. 3.47. Profile of *Indri*

The polar coordinate plot for this species is shown in figure 3.47. It is quite different from any so far described mainly because some items are recorded as zero so that others fall out as single radii or "spikes." These spikes point toward fruits, and toward leaves, flowers, and buds. There are also three large "wings" pointing toward varieties of leaping and canopy use, toward vertical supports, and toward large supports.

Avahi laniger, the woolly lemur

Very little has been reported to date concerning the locomotion or ecology of *Avahi*. Notes by Petter (1962) and Pollock (1979), reviewed by Tattersall (1982), may be considerably amplified by further publication of Albignac's research project (1981) being carried out in the field at Ampijoroa and Analabe in the Malagasy Republic. However, we are largely limited to Walker's brief description of locomotion. No film records were available.

Avahi is nocturnal and exclusively or almost exclusively folivorous. It is found both in drier (but still relatively rich), seasonally deciduous mixed forest (e.g., at Ampijoroa) in the northwest of Madagascar, and in wetter forest at higher altitude (e.g., at Analabe) on the west coast. It is generally found moving in the canopy or upper levels of the forest. Resting postures are described by Walker as typically vertical clinging ("with the tail curled up like a watch spring"), and movement is primarily saltatory and predom-

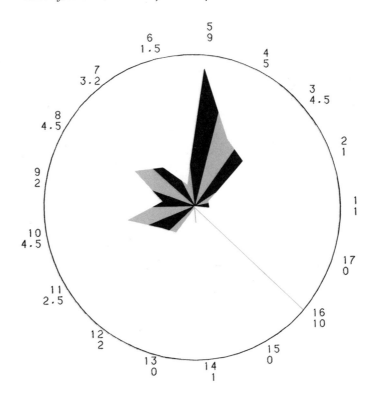

Fig. 3.48. Profile of *Avahi*

inantly between vertical supports. In these features it resembles *Indri* rather than *Propithecus*. Walker's descriptions of quadrupedal descending of trunks and bipedal hopping on the ground, however, recall *Propithecus* rather than *Indri*. And it is also recorded by Albignac as venturing into the "finest branches" to feed, which suggests a greater locomotor lability than that of *Indri*.

When more detailed studies of this species are available, it will be of great interest to reassess this picture. For if the species really does resemble *Indri* in some respects and *Propithecus* in others, then its real position would not be between the two but rather in a triangular relationship to them. Information from all anatomical studies that have been carried out so far (Oxnard 1983), supports a triangular anatomical relationship between these three forms. This is one of the ways in which morphometric studies may provide predictive data for behavioral analyses.

On these very unsatisfactory bases we have conservatively estimated a plot for *Avahi* (figure 3.48). This plot, too, is quite different from any so far described except the last. Again it is because some items are recorded as zero so that others fall out as single radii, or "spikes." A large spike points toward leaves, flowers, and buds, and a very small one toward fruit. There are again three large "wings" pointing, in this case, toward varieties of leaping and canopy, toward horizontal and vertical supports, and toward large supports, respectively.

Fig. 3.49. *Propithecus verreauxi*

Propithecus verreauxi, Verreaux' sifaka

Propithecus verreauxi (figs. 3.49 and 3.50) has been studied most extensively by Richard (1974, 1977), primarily at Hazafotsy and Berenty, Madagascar. Its behavior has been reviewed by Walker (1979), Hladik (1980), and Tattersall (1982). Film was made available by Walker, and we also used Struhsaker's and Richard's film, and Attenborough's "Life in the Trees."

The behavior of *Propithecus verreauxi* is considerably more generalized than that of *Indri*. In particular, in two of the films available to us, a marked contrast was evident in locomotion. Walker's film was made in wetter, reasonably high forest at Berenty; Richard's film at Hazafotsy, in dry scrub dominated by vertically oriented spiny Didiereaceae trees. In both cases locomotion was predominantly saltatory, but in the wet forest considerable

Fig. 3.50. *Propithecus verreauxi*

quadrupedalism was evident, particularly in the course of foraging. Again, at Hazafotsy, vertical clinging is clearly the predominant posture (at least according to the available film), but in the mixed forest, sitting postures are clearly more common than vertical clinging. Use of vertical supports is certainly high in both cases, particularly during saltatory locomotion, but at Hazafotsy, it is much more predominant.

The influence of habitat structure is considerable, in terms of both tree shape per se and the contrast between the forest with at least partial canopy cover as at Berenty, and undergrowth, as at Hazafotsy.

Differences with *Indri* are several. First, there is greater frequency of climbing and other quadrupedalism. Walking is clearly more common in *Propithecus* than in *Indri*. In *Propithecus* it appears to happen at a frequency (and possibly in a role) similar to that of walking in *Galago senegalensis*. No

Fig. 3.51. *Propithecus verreauxi* in stretched-out mid-air position.

considerable distance is covered by walking, but walking seems to form a small but regular part of foraging behavior when *Propithecus* is moving horizontally in the peripheral canopy. On large supports (15 centimeters and more) the animal quite often seems to hop bipedally. Climbing is a more frequent activity, particularly in wetter forest with partial or complete canopy. The forelimb is heavily used in propulsion.

Second, locomotion on the ground in *Propithecus* is equally by bipedal hopping or asymmetrical hopping on one or the other leg, with the body moving sideways, not by crouching or ricochetal leaps.

Third, leaping "style" is not predominantly ricochetal, but apparently equally ricochetal and "crouching." Body posture during leaps appears to be either vertical, with the arms quickly moved up to either side of the head and the hindlimbs flexed, or, on some longer leaps, almost horizontal with hindlimbs extended and arms semiflexed (fig. 3.51). Hindlimbs usually make the initial contact, but not exclusively so by any means. The tail appears to be used to aid body rotation, but not with any rapid "flicks" as in the Tarsiidae or Galaginae.

During a leap, the forelimbs may be held in a raised position, quite unlike the Tarsiidae and Galaginae, for several possible reasons: (1) to prepare for the forelimb to make first contact in some leaps, (2) to stretch the lateral skin as a gliding membrane, as Pollock suggests for *Indri* (also noted on anatomical grounds by Oxnard 1973 and 1983), and/or (3) as seen in the available films, to enable *Propithecus* to snatch at branches above their heads to slow their descent in passing during a long downward leap, and even in landing (again noted by Oxnard 1983). All of these are mechanisms that would induce tensile stresses in forelimbs in these species. Unlike the case in *Indri*, running leaps off the ends of branches were recorded occasionally in the *Propithecus* films.

There is not adequate information for an accurate overall assessment of support usage, particularly since *Propithecus* inhabits two very different habitats. Horizontal supports are used more frequently than in *Indri*, but whether more or less than verticals we cannot be sure. We have scored horizontals as being used equally commonly as in *Galago senegalensis*; but, despite the strong vertical clinging and leaping propensities of this latter species, we have given a much higher value for usage of verticals in *Propithecus* than in *G. senegalensis* because of the stress that the various authors quoted have placed upon vertical supports, and because it seems that *Propithecus* is much more specialized in its locomotor behavior than is *G. senegalensis*. Large supports do seem much more commonly used than small supports, as consideration of differences in body weight would imply.

Suspensory postures are quite common in *Propithecus*, much more so than in the galagines, especially those involving forelimb tension. Overall, both of the indriids will be subject, we feel, to particularly high tensile forces because of increased size, occasional bridging behavior, pulling in of branches, suspensory postures and suspensory episodes in and at the end of leaping, and whiplash during ricochetal leaping.

The polar coordinate plot for this species is shown in figure 3.52. This plot, too, is quite different from any so far described. As with the other indriids, this is because some items are recorded as zero so that others fall out as single radii, or spikes. These spikes point toward fruits, and toward leaves, flowers, and buds. The remaining envelope is a convex hull representing most variables to some considerable degree, especially, of course, the leaping variables.

Fig. 3.52. Profile of *Propithecus*

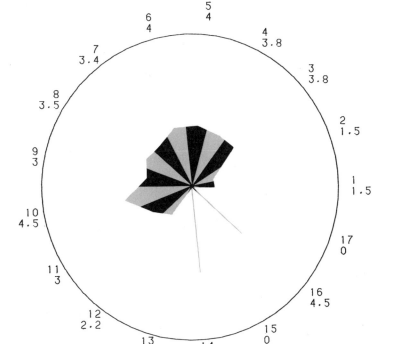

Fig. 3.53. *Hapalemur griseus*
(after a photograph by Sorby)

Lemurinae

Hapalemur griseus, the grey gentle lemur

Hapalemur griseus (fig. 3.53) has been briefly observed by Petter and Peyri-éras (1970, 1975) in the field at Maroantsetra, Madagascar, and Walker (1979) has made notes on its locomotion in captivity. Walker has made his short film section available to us. In addition, Hladik (1979) and Tattersall (1982) review this animal's behavior.

Knowledge of *Hapalemur*'s locomotion in the wild is inadequate for other than a very tentative profile, because the locomotor propensities and capabilities of the captive specimens do not give a reliable basis for an estimate of their behavior in the field. For example, support constraints must be particularly high in this species, since *Hapalemur griseus griseus* lives primarily in bamboo thickets and *H. griseus alaotrensis* in partly floating reed beds in the Malagasy lake Alaotra. The diet of *H. griseus*, according to Petter and Peyriéras, is largely composed of bamboo shoots and fruits (*H. griseus griseus*), or reed stems and leaves and fruit (*H. g. alaotrensis*). Thus, the species is likely to encounter, overwhelmingly, fairly close-packed vertical supports of medium to large size (*H. g. griseus*) or of small diameter (*H. g. alaotrensis*).

However, from available film it is apparent that *H. griseus griseus* has loco-motor propensities which, although intermediate between those of indriids and those of lemurines, are considerably closer to the latter in our opinion. Given the animal's small size, the available supports must give its locomotion in the wild indriid rather than lemurine features.

Hapalemur griseus are certainly capable of short, rapid leaps between verticals, and various authors note that they are capable of long leaps. Petter and Peyriéras, however, note that leaps of the *alaotrensis* subspecies tend to be clumsy, and that they may even fall into the water.

Hapalemur leaps to and from horizontal and oblique supports as well as vertical. Its leaping is much less stylized than either of the two indriids. Forelimbs usually make contact first in the leaps we have seen. Body posture, it appears, may be vertical, or when the leap involves a horizontal support, horizontal. *Hapalemur* can perform ricochetal leaps (but so can *Lemur catta*, see below). However, most of the locomotion filmed, concurring with the literature on captive specimens, is running, interspersed with hops that are either froglike or involve only a little forelimb contact with the ground, or climbing, or walking. On the ground, *Hapalemur* appears awkward, with rather abducted limb postures, but on a branch, a full striding quadrupedalism with hindfoot contacting the ipsilateral forefoot occurs.

In terms of posture, sitting is common on horizontal supports and so, on appropriate supports, is vertical clinging. The short forelimbs of *Hapalemur*, however, do not permit embracing of large supports and the animal must rely on surface irregularities for maintaining its grasp. Suspensory postures are also seen. Although *Hapalemur griseus griseus* must frequently use the ground to move between bamboo patches, and *H. griseus alaotrensis* can swim well (apparently one way of getting between reed patches), it is clear that the habitats of these two subspecies are likely to impose upon them locomotion heavily dependent upon climbing, vertical clinging, and leaping. We have, accordingly, so profiled them, while stressing that the plots are only tentative.

The polar coordinate plot for this species is shown in figure 3.54. There is a single spike for this species at leaves, flowers, and buds. The remainder of the plot is butterfly-shaped with wings encompassing the adjacent variables from leaping to undergrowth, and quadrupedal locomotor modes to large supports. Small supports and horizontal supports are somewhat lacking.

Varecia variegatus, the ruffed lemur

For our profile and discussion of *Varecia variegatus* (fig. 3.55), we rely on the often differing accounts of Walker (1979) and Tattersall (1982), and also employ Crompton's observations from film taken by Walker.

Compared to *Lemur catta*, and probably to other lemurs of the same ge-

Fig. 3.54. Profile of *Hapalemur griseus*

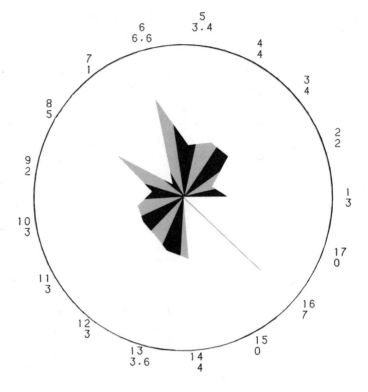

Fig. 3.55. *Varecia variegatus*

nus, *Varecia variegatus* are less saltatory, but engage more often in walking and running, with intercalated bounding gait rather like *Galago crassicaudatus*. They are inclined to use falling leaps at the end of branches, landing "spreadeagled or forelimb first if the objective is a single branch" (Tattersall), and in particular engage in frequent suspensory postures (from the hindlimb, but much less the forelimb). Sometimes, according to Tattersall, they descend from branch to branch by letting go from this position and falling (a mechanism that readily produces tensile forces in the limb as described by Oxnard 1983).

It is clear from the film and from Walker's account that they are much more hesitant and less agile leapers than *Lemur catta*. However, the captive specimens in Walker's film may not have been able to carry out their full range of natural behaviors. They seem uncomfortable in quadrupedalism on small supports (probably because of large body size, which may account for suspensory behaviors). They display a clear preference for horizontal supports over vertical.

Their detailed diet is largely unknown, but they are likely to be frugivorous. A lack of quantitative data renders our profile tentative, however. The polar coordinate plot for this species is shown in figure 3.56. This plot has its heaviest concentration on fruits, with smaller radii for (a) leaves, flowers, and buds, (b) running and falling leaps, (c) slow quadrupedalism, climbing, and large supports, and (d) horizontal supports and the canopy.

Fig. 3.56. Profile of *Varecia variegatus*

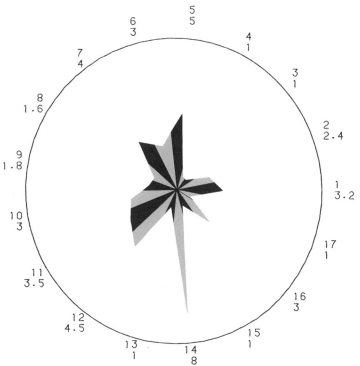

Fig. 3.57. *Lemur catta*
(after a photograph by Grzimek)

Lemur catta, the ringtail lemur

Accounts of the behavior of the ringtail lemur (figure 3.57) are presented in Jolly (1966), Sussman (1974), Budnitz and Davies (1975), Walker (1979), and Tattersall (1982). Most studies have been carried out at Berenty, Madagascar, although Sussman's study was made at Antseranomby, a rather wetter forest. Films by Walker and by Attenborough were also available to us, and we rely on Crompton's personal observations of captive specimens as well.

The diet of *Lemur catta* varies seasonally, involving fruits, leaves, and buds. In Jolly's and Sussman's studies, *L. catta* spend about 30 percent of the time on the ground, but Budnitz and Davies put their figure at less than 15 percent. *L. catta*'s behavior is very flexible, as is their locomotion; but quantitative estimates of this type among different investigators are so fraught with problems that figures as different as 15 percent and 30 percent might well be obtained from very similar behavioral sequences. Although primarily engaging in quadrupedal locomotion, either walking or climbing, and sometimes running, they readily leap between supports of any angle, sometimes in ricochetal sequences. They generally land forelimb first after a leap. But when leaping downward onto a large horizontal support or the ground, or during a series of ricochetal leaps, they land hindlimb first. Hindlimb suspension and vertical clinging are reported, but standing postures are most common.

The behavior of *Lemur catta* probably varies much according to the available supports. Thus, Sussman, working in a forest with less scrubby elements and no Didiereaceae, did not record vertical to vertical leaping. In Attenborough's film of a lemur troop moving through open woodland with abundant saplings, however, this movement occurred quite commonly. It would be difficult, then, to present a simple, accurate profile, and our plot therefore represents what at this stage we believe are likely "typical" or "overall" frequencies.

Compared to other lemurs, the frequent saltation and possibly more common suspension (excluding, perhaps, *Varecia variegatus*) may induce transitory peaks of tension bearing, but the overall quadrupedal nature of *L. catta* locomotion means that levels will not be generally high.

The polar coordinate plot for this species is shown in figure 3.58. This plot distinguishes (a) leaves, buds, and flowers, (b) fruits, (c) slow quadrupedalism, climbing, and large supports, and (d) horizontal supports.

Lemur fulvus, the brown lemur

The behavior of the *Lemur fulvus* subspecies is reportedly similar to that of other members of the Malagasy genus *Lemur* except for *Lemur catta* (Tattersall 1982). For this reason we have made a composite profile of descriptions of *L. fulvus fulvus* at Ampijoroa (Harrington 1975), *L. fulvus rufus* at Tongobato and Antseranomby (Sussman 1974), and *L. fulvus mayottensis* at Mavingoni (Tattersall 1982). We have additionally used Walker's account of *L. fulvus rufus* and film of several of the *L. fulvus* subspecies mentioned.

Lemur fulvus spends only about 2 percent of its time on the ground, and seems almost entirely confined to the canopy and main branches of the larger trees. Tattersall, providing quantitative data on support use, notes that 61 percent of supports used are horizontal, 33 percent oblique, and only 3 percent vertical. Most supports used are of medium size.

Locomotion is dominated by walking and running. Leaps up to 4 meters may be made between terminal branches, but continuous quadrupedal locomotion is preferred. Vertical supports are occasionally used in leaping, according to Harrington, but this seems an uncommon event.

L. fulvus feed predominantly on leaves but also to a varying extent on fruit most often found in the fine terminal branches of the canopy. Standing or sitting postures are most often used. Suspension seems uncommon. Tensile forces are likely to be produced by the pulling-in of the leaf or fruit-bearing branches, and by whiplash during falling leaps, and are not likely to be a major influence.

The polar coordinate plot for this species is shown in figure 3.59. The plot has five large rays: (a) canopy, (b) horizontal supports, (c) slow quadrupedalism, (d) fruit, and (e) leaves, buds, and flowers. There is also a small component toward running and falling leaps.

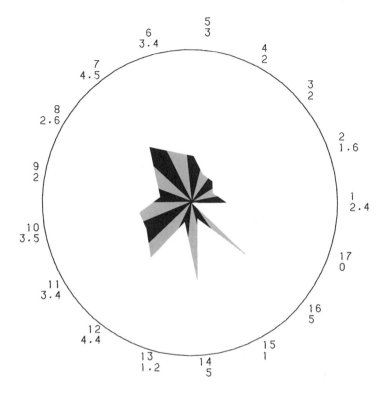

Fig. 3.58. Profile of *Lemur catta*

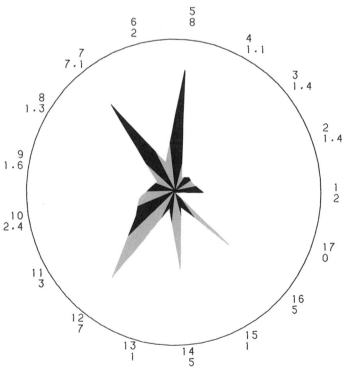

Fig. 3.59. Profile of *Lemur fulvus*

Lemur mongoz, the mongoose lemur

Our primary sources for the mongoose lemur are Sussman and Tattersall (1976) and Tattersall (1982), both field studies being carried out in Ampijoroa, Madagascar, and Walker's review of locomotion. Film of *Lemur mongoz* in captivity was made available to us by Walker.

Lemur mongoz seems to be similar to *Lemur fulvus* in many behavioral respects, so that a full account is unnecessary here. Tattersall and Sussman report that it moves "almost exclusively in the upper strata of the forest at Ampijoroa" at about 10 to 15 meters, "descending only when feeding on the lower branches of large trees or when the path of its arboreal travel demands it." Its diet involves a peculiar concentration on kapok flowers (64 percent of feeding time) and kili tree nectaries (14 percent).

Its locomotion is described by Tattersall and Sussman as differing from *Lemur fulvus* mainly in the animal's greater propensity to make branch-to-branch crossings in the canopy by leaping even when a continuous path is available. Film of captive specimens was inadequate to allow any more particular distinction of its locomotion from that of *Lemur fulvus*, and we have plotted it simply as a variant of *Lemur fulvus*-type behavior, which very possibly may be inaccurate. A connection between the dietary differences of *L. mongoz* and *L. fulvus* and their locomotor differences noted in the literature cannot be made with so little field data. The genus *Lemur* as a whole is

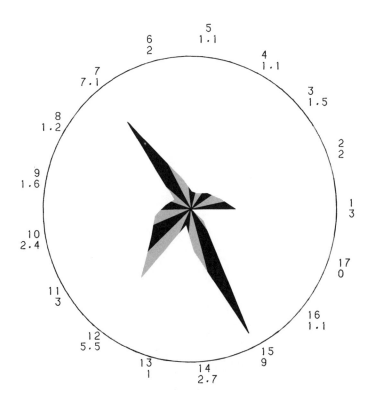

Fig. 3.60. Profile of *Lemur mongoz*

poorly known, and we have deliberately omitted discussing *L. macaco*, about which the literature says almost nothing.

Suspensory behavior and tensile activities in general are reported by Tattersall (1982) as being "common" during genus *Lemur* feeding. However, forelimb suspension is a much smaller component than pedal suspension or four-limb suspension. "Pulling-in" of food objects, such as flowers, is apparently the common method of feeding, and must be a tension-gathering activity in *L. mongoz*.

The polar coordinate plot for this species is given in figure 3.60. It has three main rays pointing to horizontal supports, slow quadrupedalism, and gums and nectar. There is a smaller ray distinguishing running leaps.

Lepilemuridae

Lepilemur mustelinus, the sportive lemur

Lepilemur (fig. 3.61) has been studied in the field by Hladik and Charles-Dominique (e.g., 1974) and by Russell (1977), who came to markedly different conclusions about ecology and energetics although working at the single site of Berenty, Madagascar. Tattersall (1982) reviews this debate and other data on *Lepilemur*, and Walker has also made observations on the locomotion of captive *Lepilemur* and produced a short film that was available to us.

Most reports of the sportive lemur's locomotion agree on the predominance of leaping. The leaps seem to be very largely of the "crouching" kind (that is, with a substantial pause between leaps and a preparatory crouch) or else ricochetal. The "typical" leap (if one can say anything from the three leaps on film and Walker's cartoon of one of them) appears to be somewhat similar to that of the indriids. It demonstrates rather late hindlimb extension after the forelimbs release their grip so that the animal "falls away" from the support somewhat before it reaches maximum acceleration. This is, again parenthetically, information that implies prior tensile forces in upper limbs.

Body posture tends to be more horizontal than for the indriid leaps we have seen. In Walker's film, the hips are almost fully flexed in flight (but see fig. 3.62 in which they are extended) and the hands are raised, as in indriids. Hindlimbs reportedly land first although we cannot confirm this. The material available to us is not adequate for a proper analysis of the leap, but on the whole, it really does seem to resemble that of the indriids. Leaps, according to Hladik and Charles-Dominique, are generally about 1.5 meters in length, rather less than those of the indriids but typical of smaller leaping prosimians. *Lepilemur* also climb vertical supports in a way similar to indriids (or tarsiers) by froglike shinning up. On the ground, *Lepilemur* moves by slow awkward walking, with rather abducted limbs and only a little ex-

Fig. 3.61. *Lepilemur mustelinus* (after photographs by Petter, Charles-Dominique, and Hladik)

Fig. 3.62. *Lepilemur mustelinus*

tension of the knee, as Walker notes. At fast speeds it hops bipedally or it leaps. This is reminiscent of *Galago garnettii* rather than indriids.

Support usage is predominantly of verticals by all accounts, although as most observations have been made in Didiereaceae forest, support *availability* is strongly biased toward verticals (see notes on *Propithecus verreauxi*, above). It would be valuable to have information from mixed forest, as *Lepilemur* is quite widespread in Madagascar. Its diet is almost entirely composed of leaves, and it rarely comes to the ground. Since the Didiereaceae forest is not very high, being scrubby, the "canopy" feature in the profile is somewhat deceptive. We do not have enough data for a fuller discussion of *Lepilemur*'s locomotor adaptation, and our profile is only a tentative one.

The polar coordinate plot for this species is shown in figure 3.63. This plot rather closely resembles that for the indriids. It has single spikes pointing to leaves, buds, and flowers, and toward fruit, respectively. There are also three "wings," one including varieties of leaping, one including vertical supports, and one including large supports.

Fig. 3.63. Profile of *Lepilemur mustelinus*

4 Activities, Habitats, and Diets for Groups of Species

Fig. 4.1. Polar coordinate plots for one example each from the plots for locomotor, habitat, and dietary variables.

In the locomotor plot, the variables are arranged anticlockwise from the three o'clock position. They are labeled with the numbers that they are assigned in Table 10, that is, running leap (1), falling leap (2), crouching leap (3), ricochetal leap (4), climbing (11), slow quadrupedalism (12), and scurrying (13). This arrangement is repeated in all the subsequent locomotor plots.

In the habitat plot, the variables are arranged anticlockwise from the three o'clock position. They are labeled with the numbers that they are assigned in Table 10, that is, canopy (5), undergrowth (6), horizontal supports (7),

The next stage in our analysis is to draw the "star" diagrams, the polar coordinate plots, for each of the locomotor, habitat, and diet sets of variables separately. This provides "reduced" polar coordinate figures for each species in each variable group (see examples in fig. 4.1).

As was done for the full polar coordinate plots of seventeen variables (described in chapter 2), these reduced polar coordinate plots were then arranged in species groups on a visual basis. Examples of such groupings are provided in figures 4.2–4.4. The groupings come not only from the broad overall similarity of the polar coordinate plot of the variables, but also from more detailed comparisons of the lengths of the radii for each individual variable. We found that we could quickly arrive at reasonably reliable and replicable sets of groups.

Of course, the most objective way of assembling such species plots is through computer techniques, specifically, multivariate statistical analysis. But for these subsets of the data, such methods did not give any different results from the visual arrangements reported here. It is only in the more

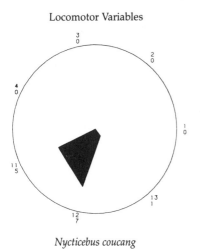

Locomotor Variables

Nycticebus coucang

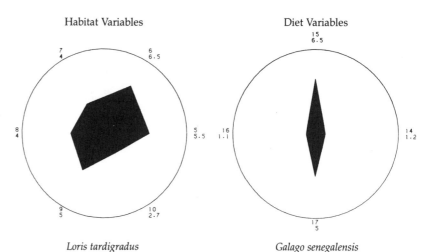

Habitat Variables

Loris tardigradus

Diet Variables

Galago senegalensis

vertical supports (8), small supports (9), and large supports (10). This arrangement is repeated in all the subsequent habitat plots.

In the dietary plot, the variables are arranged anticlockwise from the three o'clock position. They are labeled with

the numbers that they are assigned in Table 10, that is, fruit (14), gums and nectar (15), leaves, buds, and flowers (16), and animal items (17). This arrangement is repeated in all the subsequent dietary plots.

Figs. 4.2–4.4. Polar coordinate plots showing representative groups of similar plots for each of locomotor, habitat, and dietary plots. Without going into the details of the plots here, the fact that these plots do indeed form coherent groups is visually obvious.

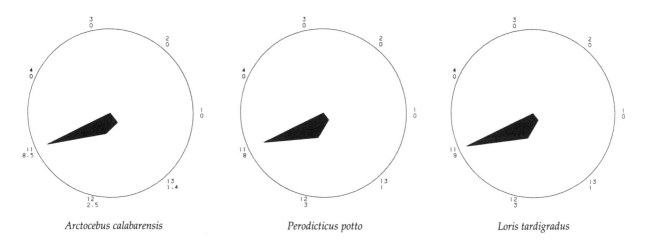

Fig. 4.2. Locomotor variables

Arctocebus calabarensis   *Perodicticus potto*   *Loris tardigradus*

Fig. 4.3. Habitat variables

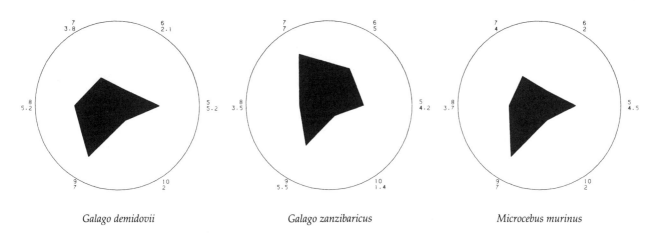

Galago demidovii   *Galago zanzibaricus*   *Microcebus murinus*

Fig. 4.4. Diet variables

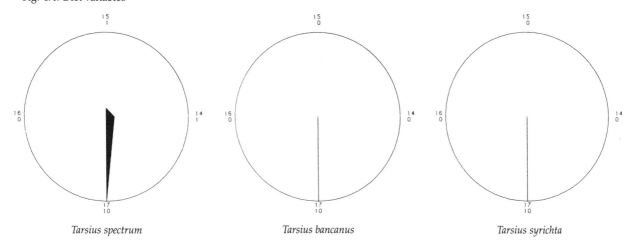

Tarsius spectrum   *Tarsius bancanus*   *Tarsius syrichta*

complex arrangements of the polar coordinate plots resulting from all variables combined, that these additional techniques are important.

Let us now, therefore, examine the three major types of variables (locomotor, habitat, and diet) separately. Such a preliminary study, we found, clarified our visual analysis of the full variable set considerably. These reduced diagrams are so easily understood, and so clear, that there is no need to describe them species by species. We can go directly to the groups that these data produce.

Species Groups Defined by Locomotor Activity Variables

Visual examination of profiles for locomotor activity variables taken by themselves reveal five very clear groups. One of these groups is large and may include three subgroups for a possible overall total of seven.

A first group of species is very readily recognized and consists of the four lorisines (fig. 4.5). They are similar because they have high frequencies for climbing. They are also similar in having considerable frequencies for slow quadrupedalism. But *Nycticebus* is a little different here in having a higher frequency for slow quadrupedalism and a somewhat lower frequency for climbing. They have extremely low or zero frequencies for everything else. This confirms the unique "slow climbing" category of most traditional locomotor classifications (e.g., Napier and Napier 1967; Oxnard 1983). It illustrates our earlier remark that, in some cases, such classifications still have their utility. However, the lorisines are an unusually distinct, coherent, and isolated grouping (see below). If we had a set of variables relating to suspensory activities, the similarities among these four species would be even greater. The grouping seen here was also readily identified in prior investigations using locomotor spectra (Oxnard, German, Jouffroy, and Lessertisseur 1981, and Oxnard, German and McArdle 1981; see also Oxnard 1983).

A second group of species consists of the three tarsiers plus *Galago alleni* and *Galago senegalensis* (fig. 4.6). The three tarsiers are, of course, very similar, and this is due to their joint possession of high values for crouching and ricochetal leaping, together with relatively equal but lower values for each other characteristic. *G. alleni* resembles the tarsiers but with even higher values for ricochetal leaping. *G. senegalensis* also resembles the tarsiers somewhat but with slightly higher values for climbing. To the degree that these profiles form a group, it consists of three central species of tarsiers and two more peripheral species of bushbaby (but each outlying in a different way). This grouping was also identified in the previous studies employing locomotor spectra as the bushbaby/tarsier group (Oxnard, German, Jouffroy, and Lessertisseur 1981, and Oxnard, German, and McArdle

Fig. 4.5. Polar coordinate plots that form a first easily recognizable group of species for the subset of locomotor variables. The variables, anticlockwise from the three-o'clock position, are labeled 1, 2, 3, and 4, and 11, 12, and 13. They comprise for each figure, in order, the sequence of running leap, falling leap, crouching leap, ricochetal leap, climbing, slow quadrupedalism, and scurrying.

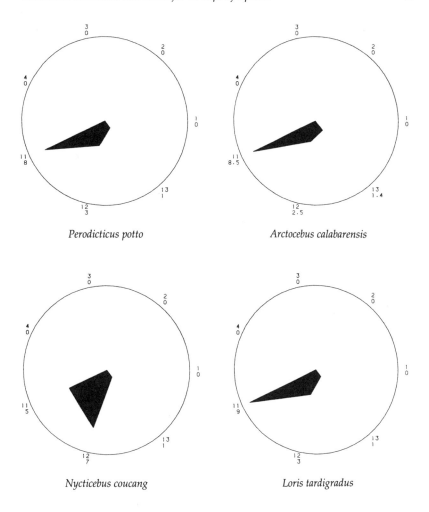

Perodicticus potto   *Arctocebus calabarensis*

Nycticebus coucang   *Loris tardigradus*

1981; see also Oxnard 1983). But in those studies the bushbabies were examined as a single genus. In the present study, where each species of bushbaby is examined separately, the majority of the bushbaby species fall into other categories.

A third group of species in the activity profiles includes *Lepilemur, Indri, Avahi,* and *Propithecus* (fig. 4.7). These are grouped together because they show very high percentages for crouching leaps and ricochetal leaps, and also because they show zero percentages for scurrying, the marked difference between this group and the previous group of tarsiers and functionally related forms. Again, the nucleus of this group is readily identified in the prior multivariate morphometric analyses (of Oxnard and colleagues). It is also not too difficult to see the most obvious part of the group (the three indriid species) in a locomotor classification: the indriid type of vertical clinger and leaper. But it takes examination at the species level and the use of

Fig. 4.6. Polar coordinate plots that form a second easily recognizable group of species for the subset of locomotor variables. The variables, anticlockwise from the three-o'clock position, are labeled 1, 2, 3, and 4, and 11, 12, and 13. They comprise for each figure, in order, the sequence of running leap, falling leap, crouching leap, ricochetal leap, climbing, slow quadrupedalism, and scurrying.

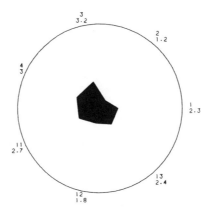

Galago senegalensis

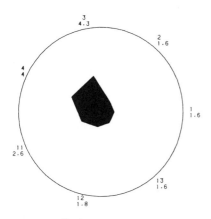

Tarsius spectrum

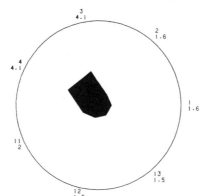

Tarsius bancanus

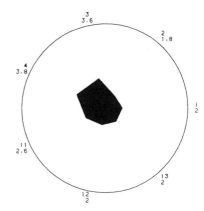

Tarsius syrichta

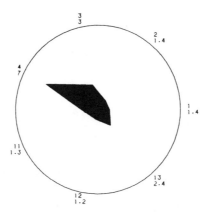

Galago alleni

Fig. 4.7. Polar coordinate plots that form a third easily recognizable group of species for the subset of locomotor variables. The variables, anticlockwise from the three-o'clock position, are labeled 1, 2, 3, and 4, and 11, 12, and 13. They comprise for each figure, in order, the sequence of running leap, falling leap, crouching leap, ricochetal leap, climbing, slow quadrupedalism, and scurrying.

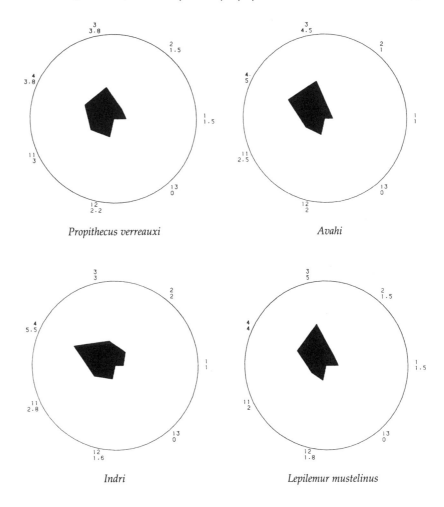

Propithecus verreauxi

Avahi

Indri

Lepilemur mustelinus

our present techniques, to be more certain about outlying or marginal members, such as *Lepilemur. Lepilemur*, based upon these new data, has, unequivocally, a locomotor activity pattern of the indriid type. Another especially interesting feature of this result is the fact that a negative measure—in this case zero percent for scurrying—is one of the major discriminators. This is a feature that is not easily incorporated into a classification.

In contrast with the profiles for the group of lemurs and related species, described below, the profiles for this group do not range across a linear spectrum. As far as can be judged, they are approximately equally different from one another, thus forming a globular-shaped cluster.

A fourth group consists of various lemurs, together with additional species. It includes *Lemur fulvus*, *L. mongoz*, *L. catta*, *Varecia variegatus*, and *Daubentonia*, along with *Galago crassicaudatus* and *G. elegantulus* (fig. 4.8). The uniting feature in all these profiles is that slow quadrupedalism and climb-ing are the most common locomotor activities. Scurrying is, in each case, relatively infrequent, and running leaps are more common than other types of leaping.

It is not with surprise that we find all the lemurs in this group. These are the forms that others have classified as "arboreal quadrupeds," even though the data show that they do practice leaping and climbing to some degrees. In addition, however, we note that two of the bushbabies are also in this group. These are *Galago crassicaudatus* and *G. elegantulus*, which we imme-diately recognize as the least specialized of the bushbabies. They do leap, indeed, but climbing and slow quadrupedalism are more common.

Again, therefore, we have defined a group, not only on the basis of an activity which is easily recognized—climbing—but also on the basis of a less obvious activity such as slow quadrupedalism. Some of the character-istics of this group have been recognized by prior locomotor classifications. Slow quadrupedalism is obviously related to the category "arboreal quad-rupeds," but other characteristics of this group have not been previously recognized. In part, this is because we are examining material at the species level, and such distinctions have been hidden by prior generic level classi-fications. But in part, it derives from our current ability, with this new ap-proach, to include far more complex combinations of variables in our loco-motor activity patterns.

Thus, this entire group forms a linear sequence of species from one end to the other. In this sequence, slow quadrupedalism gradually increases in frequency at the expense of climbing.

The remaining species are the various remaining bushbabies, the cheiro-galeines, and *Hapalemur*. They could, perhaps, be said to form a single, fifth, group. However, they are easily divided into three subsets. Their overall similarity is because they have considerable values for every param-eter; the separate subgroups can be identified by smaller differences within that overall pattern.

One subgroup is readily distinguished (fig. 4.9) because the species all possess convex envelopes. This means that there are no sudden changes in parameters as we move from one parameter to the next. This applies to *Galago demidovii, Phaner furcifer,* and *Cheirogaleus medius,* species which have a slightly greater emphasis on scurrying and running leaping than on the other parameters. The scurrying and running leaping undoubtedly merge into each other as locomotor categories in these particular species. *Galago garnettii* appears also to link with this group on the basis of the general convexity of its envelope, but its scurrying is slightly less frequent than its slow quadrupedalism or climbing.

The three species, *Hapalemur griseus, Galago zanzibaricus,* and *G. senegalen-sis,* though not very different from the foregoing, can be readily identified as a second subgroup (fig. 4.10). In addition to having intermediate values of most variables, they possess somewhat larger values for running leaping

Fig. 4.8. Polar coordinate plots that form a fourth easily recognizable group of species for the subset of locomotor variables. The variables, anticlockwise from the three-o'clock position, are labeled 1, 2, 3, and 4, and 11, 12, and 13. They comprise for each figure, in order, the sequence of running leap, falling leap, crouching leap, ricochetal leap, climbing, slow quadrupedalism, and scurrying.

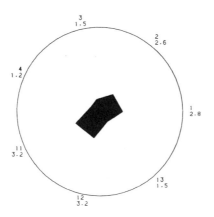

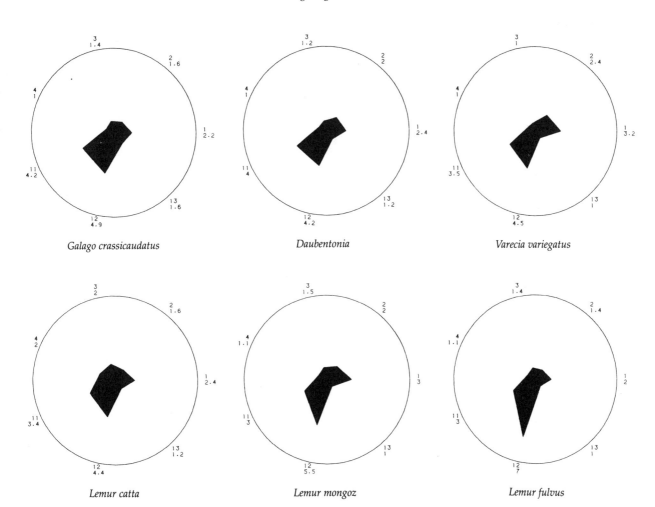

Galago elegantulus

Galago crassicaudatus   *Daubentonia*   *Varecia variegatus*

Lemur catta   *Lemur mongoz*   *Lemur fulvus*

Fig. 4.9. Polar coordinate plots that form a fifth easily recognizable group of species for the subset of locomotor variables. The variables, anticlockwise from the three-o'clock position, are labeled 1, 2, 3, and 4, and 11, 12, and 13. They comprise for each figure, in order, the sequence of running leap, falling leap, crouching leap, ricochetal leap, climbing, slow quadrupedalism, and scurrying.

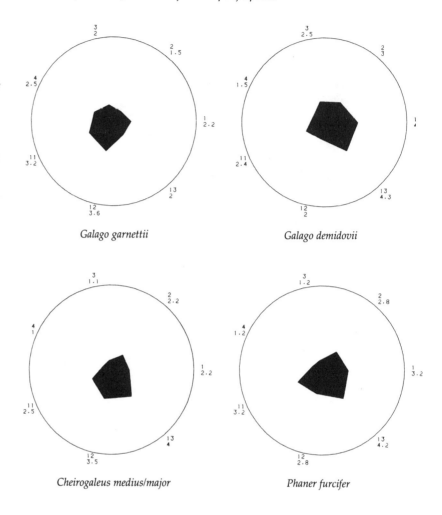

Galago garnettii

Galago demidovii

Cheirogaleus medius/major

Phaner furcifer

and crouching leaping compared with smaller values for the intermediately placed falling leaping. This produces a distinct concavity in the upper right of the profile that is common to them all. These species also show larger values for scurrying, and this emphasizes that in these particular species (but not necessarily in others) scurrying merges into running leaping and crouching leaping merges into ricochetal leaping. But the four parameters are not connected by falling leaping. In this group, falling leaping would appear to be a much more separate activity.

The last two species—*Microcebus coquereli* and *M. murinus*—are also specially distinguished as a subgroup within this larger group (fig. 4.11). Though possessing (like all the other species) values for most parameters that have little difference, they show a special reduction in ricochetal leaping that renders a concavity in the upper left of the profile. They also have relatively high values for scurrying. The implication here is that their leaping is somewhat less specialized than that of the bushbabies that are also within the overall group.

Fig. 4.10. Polar coordinate plots that form a sixth easily recognizable group of species for the subset of locomotor variables. The variables, anticlockwise from the three-o'clock position, are labeled 1, 2, 3, and 4, and 11, 12, and 13. They comprise for each figure, in order, the sequence of running leap, falling leap, crouching leap, ricochetal leap, climbing, slow quadrupedalism, and scurrying.

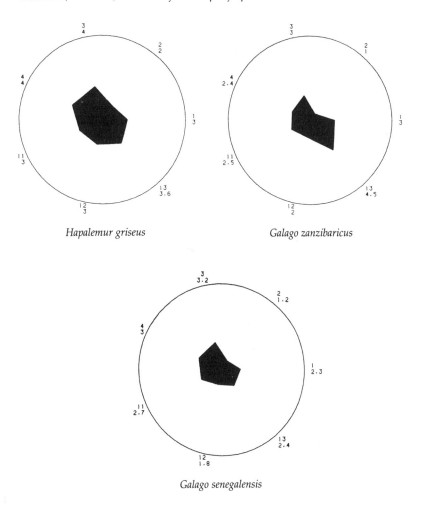

Hapalemur griseus   *Galago zanzibaricus*

Galago senegalensis

Fig. 4.11. Polar coordinate plots that form a seventh easily recognizable group of species for the subset of loco-motor variables. The variables, anti-clockwise from the three-o'clock posi-tion, are labeled 1, 2, 3, and 4, and 11, 12, and 13. They comprise for each fig-ure, in order, the sequence of running leap, falling leap, crouching leap, ricochetal leap, climbing, slow quadru-pedalism, and scurrying.

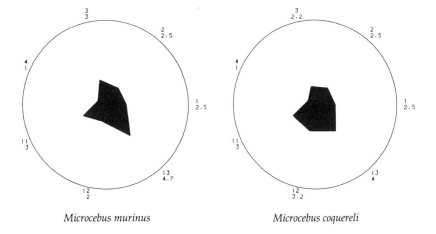

Microcebus murinus   *Microcebus coquereli*

All of these species form an overall group, but it is circular in form; there is no linear spectrum. Bushbabies tend to lie opposite mouse lemurs in this circular arrangement. The arrangement resembles part of the group of cheirogaleines in the locomotor classifications and spectra of Oxnard, German, and McArdle (1981; also Oxnard 1983). It differs, however, from that grouping because it includes the remaining bushbabies that are not closely similar to the tarsiers. This is clearly because the various bushbabies have been separated at the specific level in these studies, but were mostly grouped at the generic level in the earlier investigations.

Overall, then, these activity groupings make considerable locomotor sense and can be seen to be related, though containing much more detail, to the coarser groups of prior locomotor classifications and spectra.

What is of most interest to us now, however, is to see how the picture that they provide is related to the pictures of variables (i.e., habitat and diet) stemming from each of the other groups. Ultimately, of course, we are interested in how all three sets operate together in forming clusters of species and that is the subject of chapter 5.

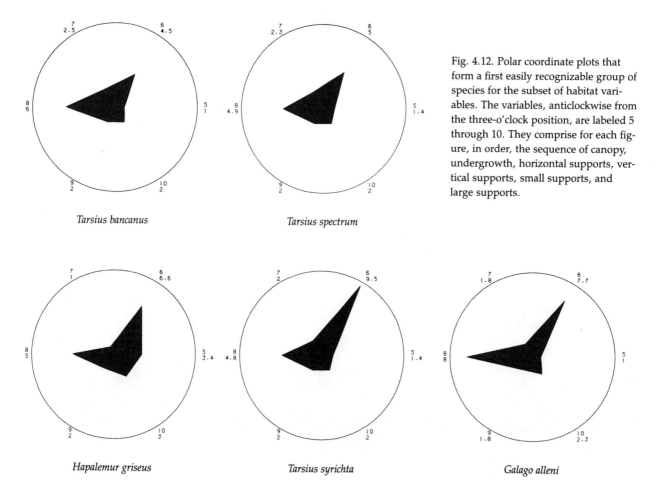

Fig. 4.12. Polar coordinate plots that form a first easily recognizable group of species for the subset of habitat variables. The variables, anticlockwise from the three-o'clock position, are labeled 5 through 10. They comprise for each figure, in order, the sequence of canopy, undergrowth, horizontal supports, vertical supports, small supports, and large supports.

Species Groups Defined by Habitat Variables

Examination of profiles for the habitat utilization variables taken by themselves reveal as many as eight groups.

One group especially easy to identify is composed of, in a linear sequence, *Tarsius bancanus, T. spectrum, Hapalemur griseus, T. syrichta,* and *Galago alleni* (fig. 4.12). This cluster arises from heavy participation of variables for undergrowth and vertical supports, together with low participation for horizontal supports. For these species there may be a close association between high values for vertical supports and low values for horizontal ones. These particular habitat profiles seem to reflect one expression of the locomotor category of "vertical clinging and leaping." They obviously relate to the characteristics of the supports available near ground level (see Crompton 1982, 1984; Crompton and Andau 1986).

A second easily distinguishable group consists of those species that share high values for canopy and horizontal supports, together with low values for most other variables (fig. 4.13). The species are *Galago crassicaudatus, Lemur fulvus,* and *Nycticebus coucang. Lemur mongoz* can be included as a marginal member of this group if we make an exception for its low participation in the canopy. The remainder of its envelope fits closer to the other members of this group than with any other group.

Fig. 4.13. Polar coordinate plots that form a second easily recognizable group of species for the subset of habitat variables. The variables, anticlockwise from the three-o'clock position, are labeled 5 through 10. They comprise for each figure, in order, the sequence of canopy, undergrowth, horizontal supports, vertical supports, small supports, and large supports.

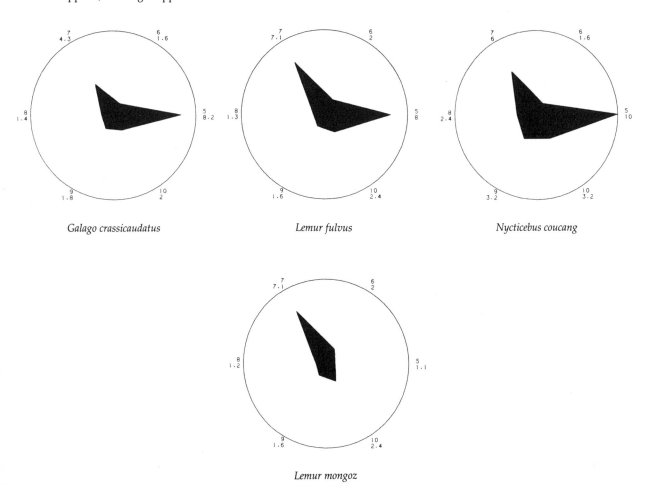

Galago crassicaudatus   Lemur fulvus   Nycticebus coucang

Lemur mongoz

Fig. 4.14. Polar coordinate plots that form a third easily recognizable group of species for the subset of habitat variables. The variables, anticlockwise from the three-o'clock position, are labeled 5 through 10. They comprise for each figure, in order, the sequence of canopy, undergrowth, horizontal supports, vertical supports, small supports, and large supports.

We note that this combination of measures is virtually the opposite of the first group. Here, too, there may be a degree of association between high values for horizontal supports and low values for vertical ones, and a general relationship between support availability and forest stratum.

A third, also easily identified, group consists of six species that have intermediate and somewhat similar values for every variable (fig. 4.14). This combination produces envelopes that are convex and of intermediate size. The group includes *Phaner furcifer, Microcebus coquereli, Daubentonia, Lemur catta, Varecia variegatus,* and *Propithecus.* Though easily identified, the group has no special features. Their mark consists of not being distinguished by these variables.

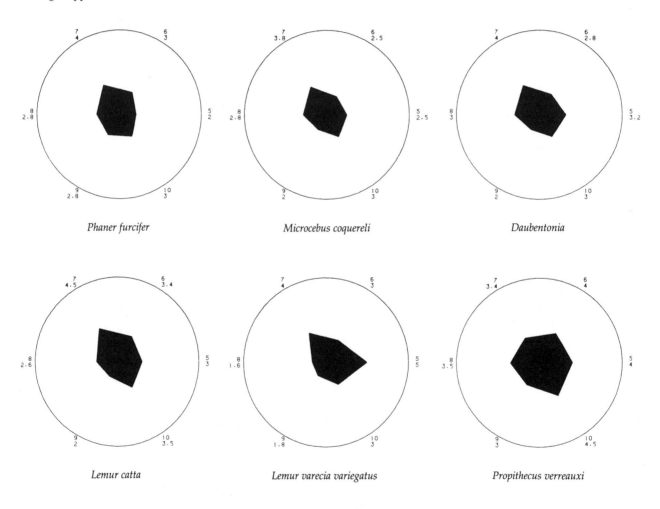

Phaner furcifer   Microcebus coquereli   Daubentonia

Lemur catta   Lemur varecia variegatus   Propithecus verreauxi

The remaining species are harder to group because there is a great deal of variability among them. A possible fourth cluster is comprised of, at first sight, the unlikely combination of *Lepilemur, Avahi, Indri, Perodicticus,* and *Galago elegantulus* (fig. 4.15). These species have similar envelopes because of sharing high values for the canopy, vertical supports, and large supports, together with some high values for horizontal supports (with the exception of *Lepilemur*).

Fig. 4.15. Polar coordinate plots that form a fourth easily recognizable group of species for the subset of habitat variables. The variables, anticlockwise from the three-o'clock position, are labeled 5 through 10. They comprise for each figure, in order, the sequence of canopy, undergrowth, horizontal supports, vertical supports, small supports, and large supports.

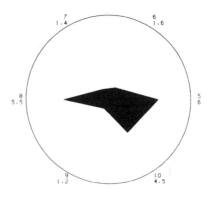

Lepilemur mustelinus

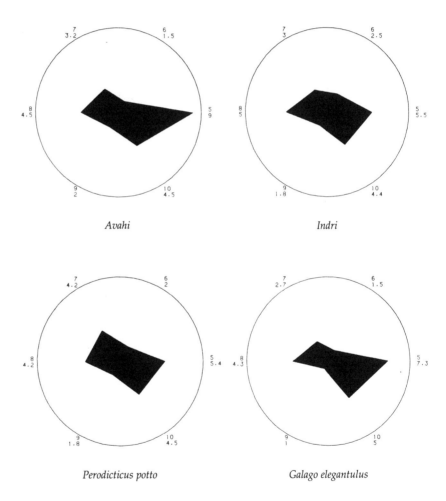

Avahi

Indri

Perodicticus potto

Galago elegantulus

In this case, we notice that high values for vertical supports do not go with low values for horizontal ones. It is a finding that entirely justifies our original decision to keep the variables separate for secondary analysis.

Despite dissimilar diets, this cluster correctly identifies a shared type of microhabitat that exists in the canopy and that contrasts with the canopy microhabitat utilized by the second group, above. *Lepilemur's* position here

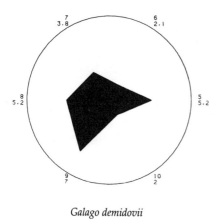

Galago demidovii

Fig. 4.16. Polar coordinate plots that form a fifth easily recognizable group of species for the subset of habitat variables. The variables, anticlockwise from the three-o'clock position, are labeled 5 through 10. They comprise for each figure, in order, the sequence of canopy, undergrowth, horizontal supports, vertical supports, small supports, and large supports.

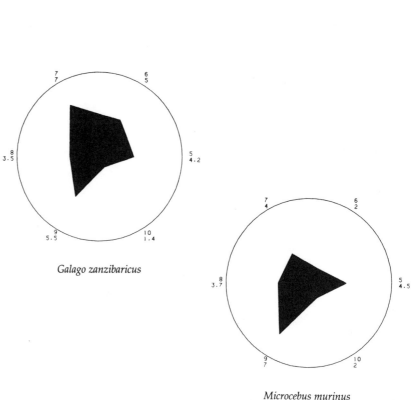

Galago zanzibaricus

Microcebus murinus

is anomalous and relates to the unique structure of its scrubby habitat in Didiereaceae forest (see species description).

A possible fifth combination includes *Galago zanzibaricus, G. demidovii,* and *Microcebus murinus* (fig. 4.16). These species are associated because of their high values for canopy, horizontal supports, and small supports. The smaller values that these species display for the other intermediately placed variables produce the characteristic shape of their envelope, with a concavity at lower right. This group differs from the immediately preceding group in that the canopy is here associated with small rather than large supports. This is, again, an important reverse correlation that justifies our keeping the variables initially separate and allowing secondary analysis to cope with statistical associations.

A possible sixth group includes *Galago senegalensis, Loris tardigradus,* and *Arctocebus calabarensis* (fig. 4.17). These species are associated primarily because they possess in common a high value for undergrowth combined with low values or moderate values for most other variables.

A final group includes *Cheirogaleus medius* and *Galago garnettii* (fig. 4.18). Though they show some similarities with one another, they could equally be linked with other groups. All that we can say here is that the data are equivocal.

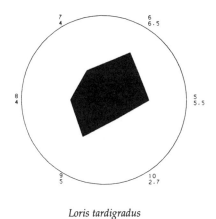

Loris tardigradus

Fig. 4.17. Polar coordinate plots that
form a sixth easily recognizable group
of species for the subset of habitat variables. The variables, anticlockwise from
the three-o'clock position, are labeled 5
through 10. They comprise for each figure, in order, the sequence of canopy,
undergrowth, horizontal supports, vertical supports, small supports, and
large supports.

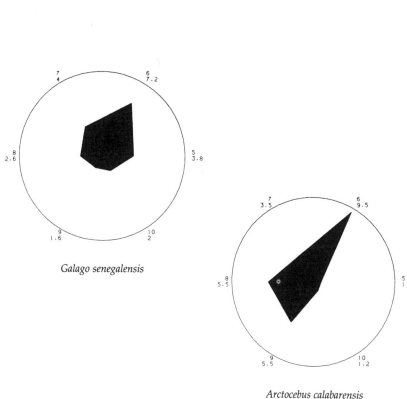

Galago senegalensis

Arctocebus calabarensis

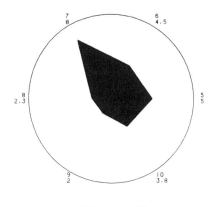

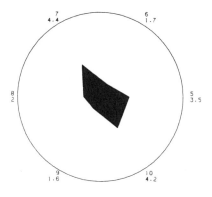

Fig. 4.18. Polar coordinate plots that
form a seventh easily recognizable
group of species for the subset of habitat variables. The variables, anticlockwise from the three-o'clock position,
are labeled 5 through 10. They comprise for each figure, in order, the
sequence of canopy, undergrowth, horizontal supports, vertical supports,
small supports, and large supports.

Galago garnettii   *Cheirogaleus medius/major*

It can thus be seen that most of these habitat groupings make biological
sense, though their patterns of clustering are somewhat less well defined
than those for the activity variables.

Species Groups Defined by Dietary Variables

Dietary variables, fewer in number and much more discrete in their description, provide the most readily recognizable groups. A first group, comprising the three tarsiers, is very easily identified by a total or almost total diet of animal items (fig. 4.19).

The second group is clearly very closely associated with the first (fig. 4.20). It displays heavy dependence upon animal foods, but also shows species eating small numbers of other items. These include *Arctocebus, Loris, Galago demidovii, Nycticebus,* and *G. zanzibaricus.* There is a linear trend here from least fruit in *Arctocebus* toward more fruit, though with still a dependence upon animal items, in *G. zanzibaricus.*

Fig. 4.19. Polar coordinate plots that form a first easily recognizable group of species for the subset of diet variables. The variables, anticlockwise from the three-o'clock position, are labeled 14 through 17. They comprise for each figure, in order, the sequence of fruit (14), gums and nectar (15), leaves, flowers, and buds (16), animal items (17).

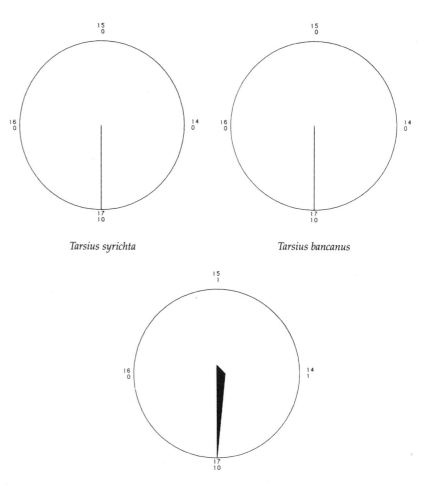

Tarsius syrichta

Tarsius bancanus

Tarsius spectrum

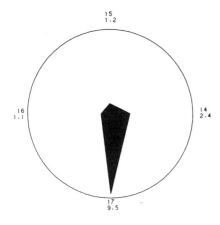

Arctocebus calabarensis

Fig. 4.20. Polar coordinate plots that form a second easily recognizable group of species for the subset of diet variables. The variables, anticlockwise from the three-o'clock position, are labeled 14 through 17. They comprise for each figure, in order, the sequence of fruit (14), gums and nectar (15), leaves, flowers, and buds (16), and animal items (17).

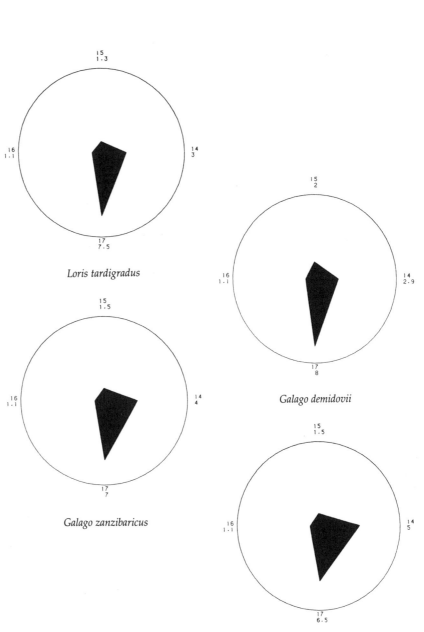

Loris tardigradus

Galago zanzibaricus

Galago demidovii

Nycticebus coucang

A third completely different group is also easily identified: those species with a total or almost total dependence upon leaves, buds, and flowers, with little to some fruit (fig. 4.21). This group includes the three indriids, together with *Hapalemur* and *Lepilemur*.

The fourth group is closely associated with the third (fig. 4.22). It is made

Fig. 4.21. Polar coordinate plots that form a third easily recognizable group of species for the subset of diet variables. The variables, anticlockwise from the three-o'clock position, are labeled 14 through 17. They comprise for each figure, in order, the sequence of fruit (14), gums and nectar (15), leaves, flowers, and buds (16), and animal items (17).

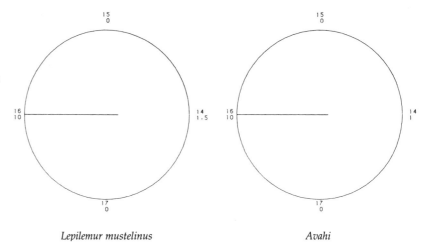

Lepilemur mustelinus   *Avahi*

Fig. 4.22. Polar coordinate plots that form a fourth easily recognizable group of species for the subset of diet variables. The variables, anticlockwise from the three-o'clock position, are labeled 14 through 17. They comprise for each figure, in order, the sequence of fruit (14), gums and nectar (15), leaves, flowers, and buds (16), and animal items (17).

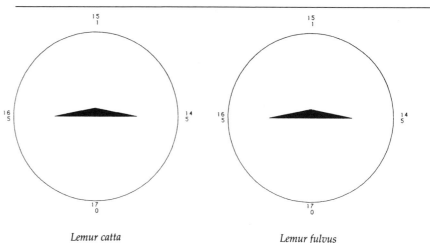

Lemur catta   *Lemur fulvus*

Fig. 4.23. Polar coordinate plots that form a fifth easily recognizable group of species for the subset of diet variables. The variables, anticlockwise from the three-o'clock position, are labeled 14 through 17. They comprise for each figure, in order, the sequence of fruit (14), gums and nectar (15), leaves, flowers, and buds (16), and animal items (17).

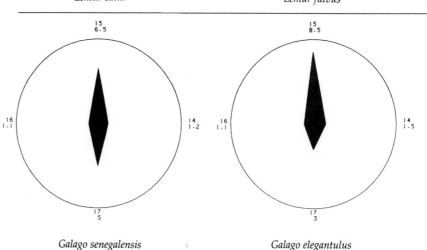

Galago senegalensis   *Galago elegantulus*

up of species that have heavy dependence upon fruit together with leaves, buds, and flowers: *Lemur catta, L. fulvus,* and *Varecia variegatus.*

The fifth group (fig. 4.23) consists of all the species that are most heavily dependent upon saps, gums, and nectar in the diet. These species are, in a relatively linear sequence, *Galago senegalensis, G. elegantulus, Phaner furcifer, Lemur mongoz,* and *G. crassicaudatus.*

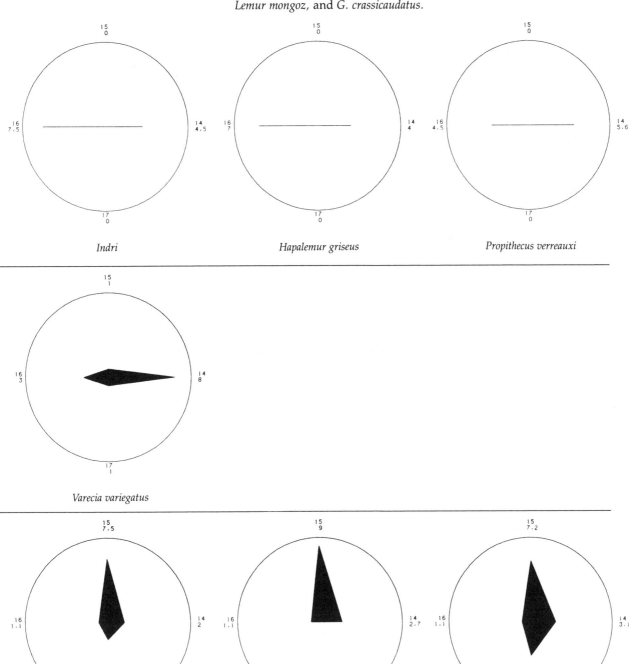

Indri   *Hapalemur griseus*   *Propithecus verreauxi*

Varecia variegatus

Phaner furcifer   *Lemur mongoz*   *Galago crassicaudatus*

The sixth and last group of species is heavily dependent upon fruit, but uses considerable amounts of various other items, especially animal foods, in the diet (fig. 4.24). It includes, in a sequence that is recognizably linear, *Daubentonia*, *Cheirogaleus medius*, *Perodicticus potto*, *Galago alleni*, and *Microcebus murinus*. Two species, *Galago garnettii* and *Microcebus coquereli* are somewhat outlying to more than one group but are perhaps closest to this last in terms of combining the eating of fruit and animal items.

It can thus be seen that these dietary groupings of species make considerable biological sense. Again, some of the groups display associations among different dietary items. Others do not. Keeping the variables separate at this stage in the analysis has allowed us to define these associations clearly.

Comparison of Activity, Habitat, and Dietary Complexes

Several comments can now be made about the investigation just described. First, the three sets of variables do seem to provide clusters of species that are biologically sensible. It is apparent that the method of display, the polar coordinate plot, makes it relatively easy to see relationships among a complex series of many variables and through many species displaying them.

The activity profiles correlate well with prior locomotor classifications, though they provide more detailed information. The habitat profiles are also linked somewhat with the locomotor classifications, as would be expected. But they show some unusual juxtapositions that give new information about degrees of association and nonassociation among variables and animals. The dietary profiles are extremely clear and supply yet another way of viewing these species.

There are overlaps and distinctions among these three views of the species. Using the total suite of information may be especially valuable in defining overall lifestyles.

An unexpected, but in retrospect, obvious, feature of the groupings is the degree to which some groups are defined as much on negative information as positive, and in which other groups are defined on intermediate (i.e., no marked presence or absence) information.

In fact, this may be an especially important aspect of these results. Visual impressions of the natural history of animals, verbal descriptions of their characteristics, and qualitative assessments of groupings will probably always underestimate the importance of "negative information" for what are probably psychological reasons. Is an herbivore an animal that eats plant foods, or one that does not eat animals? Who has ever defined a carnivore as an animal that does not eat vegetation? But visual grouping of the raw coordinate plots sees small values along a radius as easily as it sees large

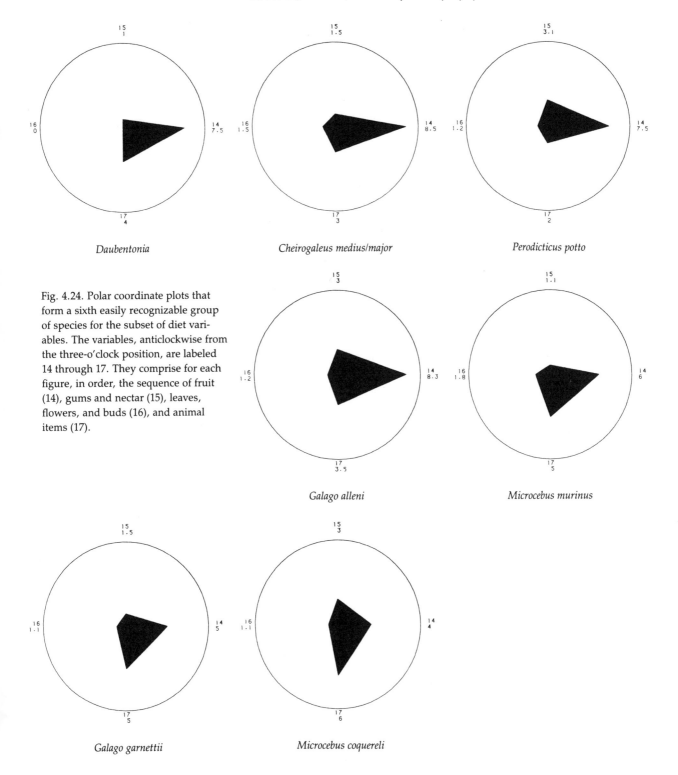

Fig. 4.24. Polar coordinate plots that form a sixth easily recognizable group of species for the subset of diet variables. The variables, anticlockwise from the three-o'clock position, are labeled 14 through 17. They comprise for each figure, in order, the sequence of fruit (14), gums and nectar (15), leaves, flowers, and buds (16), and animal items (17).

values. And Euclidean distances interpret 0 and 1 (absence and almost absence of a feature) as being as close together as 9 and 10 (almost complete presence and complete presence of a characteristic). Groupings performed in these ways are neutral to positive versus negative information. This may be an unexpected "bonus" of these investigations.

One group of species originally termed "vertical clingers and leapers" is here defined on the positive basis of frequent use of verticals and high frequency of leaping, along with negative information about other activity variables. These species, for example, generally do not perform certain activities such as scurrying, and for the most part they do not use habitats such as undergrowth and small branches. They generally prefer leaves over any other dietary items. This is descriptive of the indriid type of vertical clingers and leapers.

Other species, previously also termed "vertical clingers and leapers," differ from the above exactly because, though they do leap often and make frequent use of vertical supports, they also engage in other activities, such as climbing or scurrying. Their habitats include undergrowth or branches. They prefer other dietary items to buds and leaves. In these terms at least two other groups of "vertical clingers and leapers" are defined. One of these is the tarsiers, plus some bushbabies. A second is the cheirogaleines, plus other bushbabies. The exact relationships here need to await our study of all variables combined.

Yet other groups of species are defined because they display a mixture of intermediate levels of variables. Those species do not have especially distinctive activities, habitats, and diets, but display generalized patterns in many variables. All this is evident from the plots.

Finally, those species that are neither generalized nor specialized for any of the different leaping modes (e.g., the slow-climbing lorisines) are readily distinguished in the different sets of profiles.

In using the terms "generalized" and "specialized" we need to differentiate generalized and generalist, specialized and specialist. A species can have a generalized anatomy but be an ecological specialist, and vice versa (though less frequently so). In terms of ecological terminology, some species are stronger generalists with a narrower niche volume, others are stronger specialists, and still others are intermediate.

A second unexpected, but also in retrospect, obvious, feature of the groupings is the degree to which particular variables are closely associated in some groups, yet bear no association in other groups. Again, it is likely that our minds can readily grasp the association between a given pair of variables in some species when we assess lifestyles visually in the field or through descriptions in the literature. But we may well not easily see nonassociations between these same pairs of variables in descriptions of other species.

An example of this is the association between horizontal supports and vertical supports. As we might well expect, this association is inverse (high values for vertical supports, low for horizontal ones) in many groups, for instance, in the cluster of *Tarsius bancanus, T. spectrum, Hapalemur griseus, T. syrichta,* and *Galago alleni.* But the opposite (high participation in both vertical supports and horizontal ones) is the case in the group *Lepilemur, Avahi, Indri, Perodicticus,* and *Galago elegantulus.* The former of these is what we expect intuitively and therefore easily find. The latter is somewhat counterintuitive; we might well miss it unless it were drawn to our attention by the relative objectivity of these methods of analysis and display. There are a number of other, similar examples in these data.

What follows, now, however, and what is of most interest to us, is how all these variables are involved in helping to define the overall clusters of species. It is to this that we now turn our attention.

5   Clustering the Data Set
for Lifestyles and Anatomies

In this part of the study all variables were examined together. As for the subsets of locomotor, habitat, and dietary variables taken separately, we could identify one set of clusters by looking at the raw data using the multidimensional polar coordinate diagrams. This examination was relatively easy and replicable, and it was done with all the precautions described in chapter 2.

We also examined the data using principal components analysis as an exploratory ordination technique. Principal components analysis looks for structure in the data through the definition of a new and reduced set of dimensions. There is no reason to assume that natural clusters will be revealed by such analysis even if they are known to be "real" (i.e., taxonomic groups). The main use of the analysis here is to generate hypotheses about the niche groups.

In addition to the visual clustering technique, we also used two computational clustering methods (dendrograms and minimum spanning trees) to examine the arrangement of the species within the multivariate space.

Our particular dendrogram was generated using a Euclidean distance index and a flexible sorting strategy (Clifford and Stephenson 1975; Goodall 1973). (An unweighted group mean clustering algorithm did not result in a significantly different dendrogram, Gower 1967; Gower and Ross 1969.) Dendrograms are a useful way of getting a first impression about the possibility of groupings within the data.

Dendrograms have a problem, however, in that the links they display frequently hide clustering in the next nearest species. Thus, one cannot tell from inspecting a dendrogram alone, whether a species that links with one group is next nearest to or most distant from the next group. This is inherent in the unidimensional nature of the dendrogram. This problem can only be solved by examining the totality of the Euclidean distances and noting where misleading representations are given.

This is demonstrated in figures 5.1 and 5.2, using simple theoretical data. Figure 5.1 shows two groups, A and B, and it particularly draws attention to specimen 1, which is almost intermediate between A and B. The visual impression is that 1 belongs with A because of the overall arrangement. However, in terms of some dendrogram methods, 1 belongs with B because it is slightly closer to the nearest specimen of B. This is shown in figure 5.2. The dendrogram also suggests that specimen 1 is linked with B on the far side of B. This gives the wrong impression that 1 is nowhere near A. In fact, 1 could have been drawn in the position shown by the dashed line and 1',

Fig. 5.1. Two groups of theoretical data are plotted against two axes. The points have been carefully chosen so that point 1 is closer to one of the points in group B than it is to any of the points in group A. Yet all the next nearest distances of point 1 are with all of the points in group A. In other words, notwithstanding the minimum link with group B, point 1 belongs, visually, with group A. All of this would be much more difficult to see if the data were really in many dimensions, instead of just the two shown in the figure.

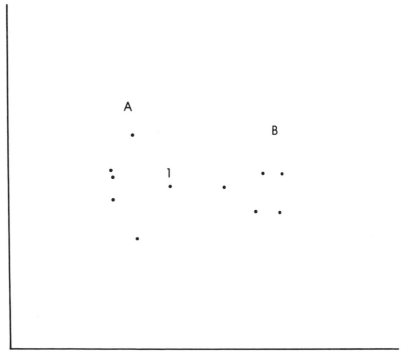

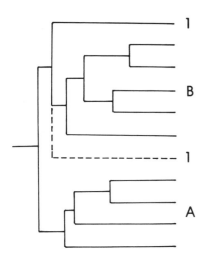

Fig. 5.2. A dendrogram that can be derived from the plot in figure 5.1. Because point 1 has a single minimum link with group B, the dendrogram links it to group B. And it does so in such a manner that it is not immediately apparent that it is also closer to group A than any of the other points in group B. The dashed position of point 1 (for any point in a dendrogram can be rotated around its position) would make its real position a little more apparent. However, in more complex dendrograms, this cannot always be done (see fig. 5.6 for a real example).

which would have given a better impression of the true relationship of the specimen to the groups.

When we have only two groups then, we obviously would draw the dendrogram with 1 in the new (dashed) position. But when there are more than two groups it may not be possible to do this because other groups may intervene between A and B. This is one of many problems of using the one-dimensional dendrogram to understand the nature of groups, and is often not appreciated by those who read about this method.

In addition, the dendrogram does not easily take into account the "limits" of the distances that it uses. Thus, a link that is slightly shorter than three others may not be statistically any shorter because all four links may have statistical limits that include each other. Felsenstein (1984) attacks this problem statistically; Oxnard (1987:207) gives it an intuitive, geometric description.

The second group visualizing technique that we used is the minimum spanning tree. This was calculated from the principal components analysis and plotted in the plane of the first two components. Minimum spanning trees avoid some of the problems of the dendrogram that result from the dendrogram's essentially unidimensional method of display.

But even minimum spanning trees have disadvantages. One is that it is not easy to see the next nearest links. These next nearest links may actually be more important in defining groups, especially when they are close to the minimum links. They may, in fact, better define the groups that are present than the minimum links.

This is shown in another example using the same theoretical two-dimensional data. In figure 5.3, the two-dimensional arrangements of groups A and B and the somewhat intermediate specimen 1 are again shown. The formation of the minimum spanning tree is illustrated in figure 5.4, but it has been stopped short at the point where specimen 1 was linked into the system. By stopping at that point, we see that 1 links with group B because the distance to one of the specimens of group B is its minimum link. But when we place all of 1's next nearest links—the dashed links—in the diagram, we see clearly that, despite the existence of the single minimum link with group B, 1 really belongs with the A group.

Groups are best defined by looking at a large number of links. In the process of recognizing groups, consideration of near minimum links may indicate "groupiness" by providing some notion of the density of links within the data space. If one species has a nearest link with a single species in a first group, but has seven next nearest links with seven of the species of a second group, then it is the second group to which that species is most closely linked. The minimum link provides misleading information in that case.

Some of these problems are probably best solved by using methods that actually visualize many more links than merely the minimum ones. One such method is the simplicial decomposition, and another is the barycentric reduction (Oxnard and Neely 1969; Oxnard 1973). The applications of methods like these are some of the next studies that we will carry out to examine further the existence of groups in these data.

Given all these caveats, however, the main groups perceived in these data by these statistical procedures are essentially similar to those defined by the visual grouping of the polar coordinate diagrams. The visual grouping assumes no prior groups. Principal components analysis also does not assign a priori groups, nor does it weight any one variable over another. It is not surprising that the visual clusters are generally confirmed by principal components analysis. If they were not generally confirmed, we might have argued either that the visual groupings were inaccurate, or that, in reality, there were no clear groups. Happily, that discussion is rendered moot by the findings.

Once these groups have been defined by the various methods, the relationships among them are then best studied using canonical variates analyses. Canonical variates analysis, like principal components analysis, is a dimension-reducing technique. It can be used in a hypothesis-free mode for revealing the structural relationships among groups that are already known to exist. It can also be used as a hypothesis-testing technique for the statistical significance of the differences between a priori groups. We have used it here as an ordination technique by plotting the canonical scores of the different groupings within the first three canonical axes. We have also attempted to discuss their biological interpretations.

Fig. 5.3. This figure repeats the theoretical data of figure 5.1, showing two groups (A and B) with point 1 slightly closer to one point in B but in reality rather close to every point in group A.

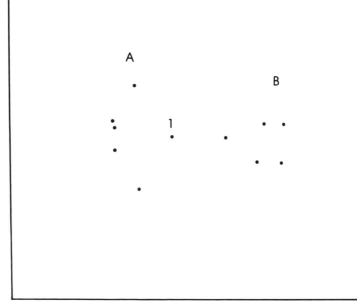

Fig. 5.4. A minimum spanning tree constructed up to the point at which it links point 1 into group B. Group A has also been outlined by the minimum spanning tree. The dashed lines show all of the next-to-minimum links of point 1; they are all with group A. The links of point 1 with group B are all far longer than these. It is thus apparent that the minimum spanning tree actually misleads by suggesting that point 1 belongs with B. Sketching the next set of minimum links—the dashed links in the diagram—corrects the misimpression (see fig. 5.7 for a real example of this difficulty).

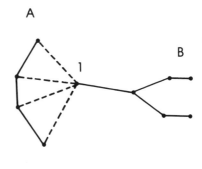

The chief difference between the principal components and canonical variates analyses, however, is in the testing. Though the niche groups are partially revealed by the principal components analyses, it is only in the canonical variates analyses that the significance of the separations of the different groups can be evaluated.

The full multivariate description of all these results is given in Lieberman, Crompton, and Oxnard (1989). But the main summary of the pattern of groupings resulting from the multivariate studies is described here.

The Five Main Lifestyle Clusters of Species

When all variables are taken together, five major groups are readily apparent. They include the following mixed series of species and genera:

1. the Lorisinae;
2. the galagos, excluding *Galago alleni* and perhaps *G. senegalensis*, together with the cheirogaleines with the exception of *Phaner*;
3. the tarsiers, with the possible addition of *Galago senegalensis* and *G. alleni*;
4. the indriids, plus *Lepilemur* and possibly *Hapalemur*;
5. the Lemurinae, plus *Daubentonia* and possibly *Phaner*.

This is the pattern of groupings that is evident from the visual clusters of polar coordinate groupings as shown by the figures as each individual group is examined. The groupings are shown in figure 5.5 in diagrammatic form.

The pattern of groupings emerging from the dendrogram study is shown in figure 5.6. Five groups are clearly evident, but they are not completely the same as those in the visual clustering. However, most of the differences are due to factors such as those to which we have just drawn attention.

For example, the dendrogram shows a first group of tarsiers plus *Galago alleni*. But *G. senegalensis*, which was also clustered with them by the visual analysis, seems very far distant in the dendrogram. It lies almost halfway down the column of species. But examination of the entire matrix of Euclidean distances shows that this is a misconception of its position. Though it is true that, on the basis of the Euclidean distances, *G. senegalensis* has its single shortest link with the group containing *Phaner, Lemur mongoz,* and the two galagos, its several next nearest links are all with the three tarsiers and *G. alleni*. It is thus with these latter that it is most fully congruent. Similar findings apply to other aspects of the links and are more fully discussed in Lieberman, Crompton, and Oxnard (1989).

In the same way, the pattern of groupings evident in the minimum spanning tree suggests similar groups of the visual comparisons, but it also needs elaboration (see fig. 5.7). Here, the nature of the display is such that

Fig. 5.5. Visual grouping of the raw data for the niche metric plots. This grouping diagram displays only the way in which the various polar coordinate diagrams (of chapter 3) for the different species are grouped. The number of such plots prevents their being shown in a single figure. They are displayed, however, group by group, in later figures. Though less rigorous than other methods of group finding, the visual method does allow groups to be recognized fairly clearly.

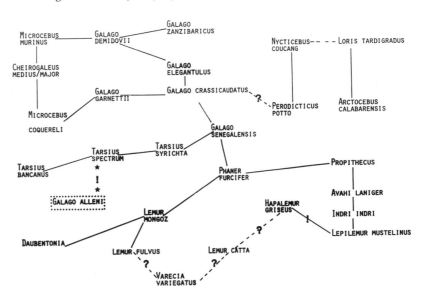

Fig. 5.6. Dendrogram grouping based upon Euclidean distances for the niche metric data. This grouping diagram also displays the main groups. As explained in the text, however, such a diagram actually hides many important relationships. Thus, though *Galago senegalensis* appears far down the list of genera, apparently a long way from the tarsiers and Allen's bushbaby, most of its links (though not its absolutely shortest link) are with that first group of tarsiers and Allen's bushbaby). Though more rigorous than a visual grouping method, this technique does not display how species are placed in relationship to groups.

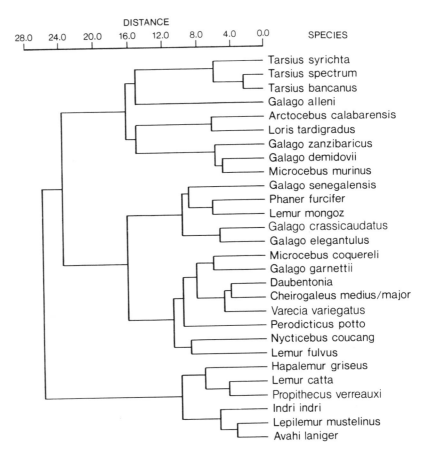

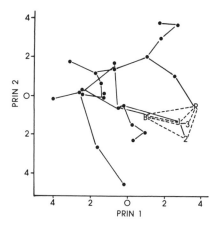

Fig. 5.7. Minimum spanning tree grouping derived from a principal components analysis, and figured superimposed upon a plot of the first two principal components. This mode of analysis also does not clearly display groups because each species is eventually joined up in the single minimum spanning tree. Again, as in the text, to take the group of tarsiers as an example, though each of the two species of *Galago* (*senegalensis* = B, and *alleni* = R) is actually linked first through a minimum link to some other species, the majority of the next nearest links of these two species are with the various tarsiers (1, 2, and 3). This is shown by dotted lines in the tree (although, of course, these dotted lines are not the "correct" length; they cannot be the correct length because the plot is only two dimensional). Thus, the three tarsiers plus the two bushbabies are a reasonably coherent group. Though more rigorous than a visual grouping method or the dendrogram display, this technique still does not include, in its grouping algorithm, those many other links that are near minimum and which contribute largely to the recognition of groups.

groups are not defined, but relationships between the species can be seen. Again, problems are evident.

To choose the same example, the three tarsiers are evident as far outliers in the minimum spanning tree. In this case, both *Galago alleni* and *G. senegalensis* are actually minimally linked with other species: *G. alleni* to an indriid, and *G. senegalensis* to *Phaner*. But consideration of next nearest links (and some are shown in the diagram [fig. 5.7] as dotted lines) places both of these genera as part of the assemblage of tarsiers. This is easier to see in the minimum spanning tree than was the case for the dendrogram because the additional links can be identified (by dotted lines) in the diagram. However, these near minimum links cannot be drawn at their "correct" lengths in a two-dimensional plot because of the multidimensional nature of the space in which they truly lie.

Neither the dendrogram nor the minimum spanning tree are especially good. Both require examination of many next nearest links. Additional clustering methods need to be applied to cover problems like these.

Finally, however, the existence of these clusters is evident in the plots of the first four principal components. These essentially confirm the visual groupings (fig. 5.8). They emphasize, however, an overlap between groups 2 and 5 that was, perhaps, not clearly apparent from the visual clustering.

The structural relationships among these groups, once defined, are demonstrated visually and significantly in the canonical variates analysis of the same data (fig. 5.9). All three of these canonical axes are highly significant, the fourth is not. Four groups are clearly separated. Again, the existence of a closer relationship between groups 2 and 5, suggested by the principal components analysis, is evident.

Clusters relating to body weight, taxonomy, and niche

Additional multivariate morphometric analyses, both canonical variates analyses and principal components analyses, were also carried out. These allow us to examine other relationships within these data. It has been suggested many times, for instance, that body-weight relationships may be closely related to locomotion, habitat, and diet. And it appears obvious that taxonomic groupings should be studied because the animals genuinely belong in a series of related taxonomic groups. Finally, the grouping of the variables by the species may also give insights into the situation.

The first of these additional studies is a canonical variates analysis showing the relationship of these data to the different body-weight classes of species (fig. 5.10). The body-weight classes are determined by information about body weight that is external to the analysis. The result demonstrates important points that bear upon the interpretations of the primary clusterings of the species.

Fig. 5.8. Primary multivariate statistical groupings revealed in the niche metric data: the principal components plots of the first four axes (two bivariate plots of the first principal component against the second, and the third against the fourth). Each group of species is indicated with large numbers from 1 to 5 and is outlined by its perimeter. The groups are distinct save for a small degree of overlap between groups 2 and 5.

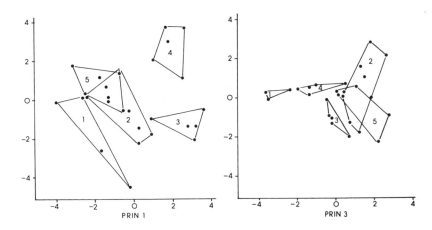

Fig. 5.9. Primary multivariate statistical separations of the groups previously revealed in niche metric data: the canonical variates analysis of the data plotted in the first three canonical axes. Each group of species is indicated with large numbers from 1 to 5 and represented by different symbols. The separations are now very clear though the closer relationship between groups 2 and 5 is still evident.

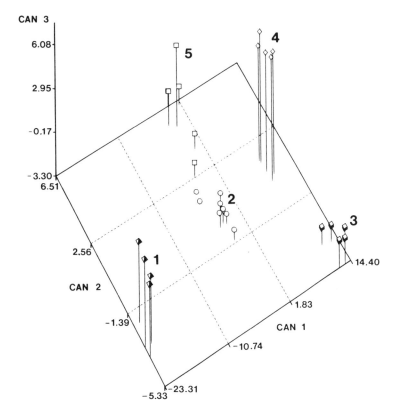

Fig. 5.10. Secondary multivariate statistical groupings of the niche metric data. This figure displays the canonical variates plot of the first three axes of the niche metric data when body weight categories (increasing body weight from A through F) are used for clustering the species. Each weight group, A through F, is represented by a different symbol.

Only the first canonical axis is performing significant overall separation. Thus the groups are far less clear than might be suspected by merely looking at the diagram. There is only one body weight separation (of weight group D from all of the others) that is highly significant. In this case, and in comparison with the analysis based upon family, it is perhaps surprising that a clear trend from A to F (small to large) does not emerge (and see text).

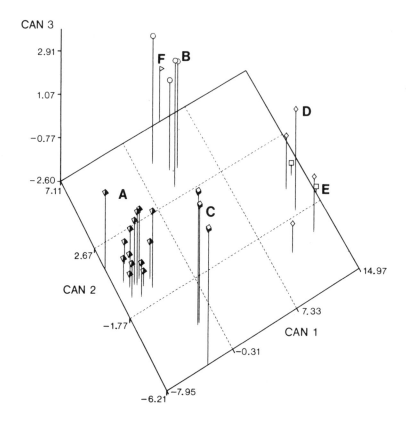

Thus, this particular analysis shows that, perhaps contrary to intuition, there is no linear trend at all in the arrangement of the weight classes of animals. Bearing in mind that only the first axis is statistically significant in this study, we can examine the separations performed in the light of that axis. In passing from the smallest group in the diagram (A) to the largest (F), we first move positively (toward the right) along the first axis to the next smallest group B, then negatively (back toward the left) on the first axis to group C, then positively (to the right again) to D, then negatively (back a little) to E, and finally negatively again (back a considerable amount to the left) to F in a position that differs little from that of B, the second smallest group.

Let us be clear. This result does not mean that size is not important. Size has some significant effects here. But we can affirm that there is no simple, linear, or monotonic relationship between size and these data. Probably what these results reflect are (a) some size relationships that are closely associated with lifestyles for some animals, (b) some size relationships that are scarcely associated at all with lifestyles for other animals, and perhaps (c) some that show intermediate associations. Size is obviously important. But it participates in such a complex manner, when viewed over such a

Fig. 5.11. Secondary multivariate statistical groupings of the niche metric data. This figure displays the canonical variates plot of the first three axes of the niche metric data when taxonomic group is used for clustering the species. The superfamilies are surprisingly well separated. Symbols for the groupings are as follows: Cheirogaleidae–pyramid; Daubentoniidae–circle; Indriidae–cube; Lemuridae–diamond; Lorisidae–square; Tarsiidae–flag.

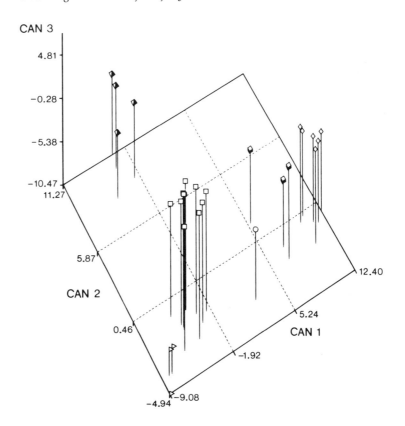

wide range of species, that it cries out for further detailed analysis of its own. We hope further investigations of size in relationship to data of this type will eventually be completed.

The second additional study is a canonical analysis of the relationships between these data and taxonomic (Family) supergroupings of the species. Like the size groups, the taxonomic groupings are also real groupings, determined by observers and data external to the analysis. They are, thus, an appropriate set of groupings to examine with this technique (fig. 5.11). The result shows, and it is generally counterintuitive, that there are unexpected and almost certainly important higher taxonomic separations of species in the data.

If there is a high association across the anatomical/lifestyle interface, such a relationship between taxonomy and lifestyles would be expected given that anatomy alone is what has been most used in the past to determine taxonomic groups. But that the lifestyle information by itself should provide such clear taxonomic separations is not immediately obvious. It is certainly not obvious in the raw data. It is only revealed when the taxonomic clusters are separated multivariately.

The third examination is a principal components analysis that tells us

Fig. 5.12. Secondary multivariate statistical groupings of the niche metric data. This figure displays the principal components plot of the first three axes for the analysis of niche metric data when the variables are grouped. It shows that the variables are not randomly mixed or without coherent structure. In fact, there is an almost complete separation between habitat variables (which are generally placed near the top of the plot) and locomotor variables (generally placed near the bottom). The dietary variables are especially interesting. Each is markedly separated from the others; each is placed at a different periphery of the entire plot. All three of the axes are used in achieving this result.

The habitat variables are represented by squares, the locomotor variables by circles, and the dietary variables by flags.

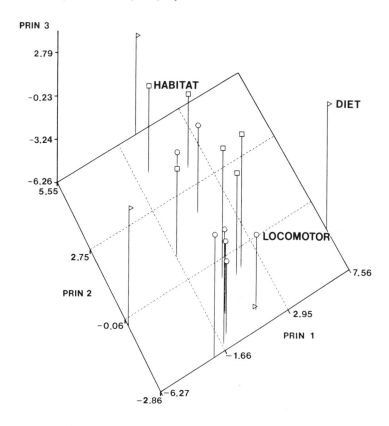

something about the relationships among the various lifestyle variables. There is no a priori arrangement of lifestyles variables that we might have guessed would exist. This is the reason why a principal components analysis is the pertinent one. The result shows, however, that there are some distinct clusters of variables (fig. 5.12).

The habitat and locomotor variables, generally, do indeed separate into two groups, though yet with a degree of overlap. Perhaps this is as we might have expected. But the dietary variables are very curiously arranged. Each one falls on the periphery of the cluster of all the variables, in a position that is separated as widely as it could be from the others (see fig. 5.12).

At a more detailed level, many interesting relationships can be seen among these variables. For example, a diet highest in gums and nectar is associated with scurrying in general terms. A diet highest in animal items is associated with undergrowth and small supports. A diet highest in fruit is associated with canopy and horizontal supports. A diet of leaves, buds, and flowers is closest to leaping and large supports. All these combinations make good biological sense and further strengthen our confidence in the data and the analyses that have been performed.

These multivariate statistical examinations hold the greatest interest at a more detailed level. At this time, however, a more complete discussion of them is provided by Lieberman, Crompton, and Oxnard (1989). They will not be examined further here, other than to note that they provide appropriate multivariate corroboration of the existence of the main groups of species identified on the basis of the raw data. It is on the biological implications of the principal clusters of species so determined that we concentrate below.

Biological relationships within the groups

Individual associations within these groupings are obviously subject to error, particularly for the less well-known species. Certainly, the particular selection of variables used influences the groupings. We have taken account of what little is known about both rare species and poorly defined variables. Indeed, one most important set of variables, to do with tension-bearing in the limbs, has been omitted entirely. Yet the arrangements that we have found seem to reflect some important biological relationships.

In particular, the arrangements further underline the observation previously made in multivariate and other analyses of prosimian limb anatomy, that at least three groups exist within leaping prosimians (Oxnard, German, Jouffroy, and Lessertisseur 1981; Oxnard, German, and McArdle 1981; Oxnard 1983). These groups relate both to biomechanically different modes of leaping, and to the support characteristics of the strata occupied. And we are gradually learning more about how these particular niche variables are themselves related.

It is of considerable interest that the separations of these three groups when examined at the coarse level of genera, using locomotor classifications or spectra, is somewhat different from these studies where they are examined at the species level, using the finer profiles of activity, habitat, and diet. The primary difference is that though some of the bushbabies group with the tarsiers, as was found in prior studies, others are closer to the cheirogaleines. It is the increased amount of detail among various species of bushbaby in complex locomotor habitats, rather than the lesser amount of detail in simple locomotor grades and coarser genera, that allows this to be seen.

Although at this stage, we have no anatomical studies that have been performed with the present lifestyle investigations in mind, there are several earlier anatomical investigations that we can use to examine the association between lifestyle profiles (niche metrics) and anatomies (morphometrics).

Two morphometric investigations, of the prosimian hip and thigh (the specific anatomical engine of leaping) and of overall limb proportions in prosimians (the structural mechanism of locomotion more broadly defined), have been undertaken at taxonomic levels fairly close to those used here. The original investigations are described in Oxnard, German, and McArdle

(1981) and Oxnard, German, Jouffroy, and Lessertisseur (1981). The work is more completely summarized in Oxnard (1983).

Although those earlier investigations gave detailed information at the species level for most of the groups, because the only behavioral information that was available was at the coarser grade of the locomotor classification, there was nothing with which to compare the detailed results. Accordingly, the details of morphometric relationships (anatomies) at the species level have not hitherto been published. Now that we have the lifestyle profiles available for species, however, it is possible to make the more detailed comparisons. The internal structure of the lifestyle (or niche) groups that emerge from the present study can be immediately and rather directly compared with the internal structure of the anatomical groups that were evident in the earlier morphometric investigations.

There also exist many other morphometric investigations of primates (e.g., of overall bodily proportions, of pelvic and scapular form, of the arm and forearm, and so on; see the full range of studies of primates of Oxnard and colleagues, Oxnard 1983). In general, these studies do provide a great deal of information about functional adaptation in prosimians. For the present purposes, however, their use is more limited because they were carried out at the generic rather than the specific level. They cannot, therefore, be compared with the present niche metric results.

First Group: The Lorisinae

Lifestyles

The lorisines (figs. 5.13 and 5.14) provide some interesting results. All four species show similar large "gaps" in their profiles (linked variables rated at or near zero) for almost three-quarters of their plots. They also show special individual "spikes" (variables that are highly rated and that are surrounded by others rated at zero). Consideration of the plots together show that there are two strongly linked pairs, one of small gracile forms (*Loris* and *Arctocebus*); one of robust, larger bodied species (*Nycticebus* and *Perodicticus*). Of each pair, the more extreme profiles are for the potto and the angwantibo.

Loris and *Arctocebus* are very similar, both relying heavily on climbing, using vertical supports somewhat more often than horizontal ones, and with a diet heavily concentrated on animal prey. We know, of course, that anatomically they are rather similar, with *Arctocebus* the more specialized of the two (e.g., in reduction of digits), as indeed it is behaviorally more specialized.

In the same way, *Nycticebus* and *Perodicticus* are rather similar. But *Nycticebus* is distinguished by a greater use of the canopy, greater dependence upon animal diet, more frequent slow quadrupedalism, and the use of more

Fig. 5.13. Raw data polar coordinate plots for the lorisines. Overall similarities and detailed differences are visually obvious.

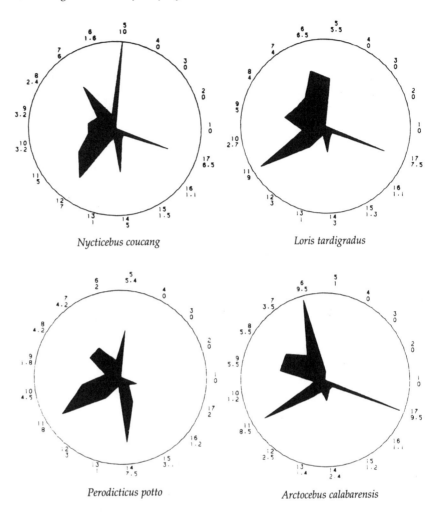

Nycticebus coucang

Loris tardigradus

Perodicticus potto

Arctocebus calabarensis

horizontal supports. Anatomically, again, they are very similar. There is, however, not a strong linkage between the profiles of the two pairs. Both of our "control" visual groupers and the computer-produced dendrogram linked the two gracile forms, very distantly with the tarsier-*Galago alleni* group.

In terms of locomotion, the two groups, gracile lorisines and tarsiers, are distinct. The plots indicate two alternative locomotor strategies for adapting to a similar forest stratum. Both the gracile Lorisinae and the tarsier group are particularly characterized by almost exclusive use of the undergrowth. Both are highly dependent on animal food. Both use vertical supports more often than horizontal supports. Small body size and gracile limb proportions are yet another similarity. The gracile lorisines have a heavy dependence upon climbing, the tarsiers on crouching leaping and ricochetal leaping. The gracile lorisines, too, utilize small supports much more often than large ones.

Thus, these two groups, the gracile lorises on the one hand and the tarsiers on the other, in adapting to the same forest stratum, have entered two very different microhabitats. The undergrowth in the tropical forest contains both closed and open phases. The closed phase consists of small localized foliage tangles of fine branches ("fine branch niche"), which spread out densely at all angles, but are closely packed. The open phase consists of what Crompton (1984) has described as the "low" or "tree trunk and ground" zone. Since neither zone contains abundant fruit or other high-fiber dietary items, in the tropical rainforest (we discuss the apparent exception of *Galago alleni's* fallen-fruit niche below) arthropods become a staple.

We suggest that tarsiers (possibly as though a tarsier were a primate "owl," following Niemitz 1984a) have adopted their unique high-speed, saltatory locomotion to allow rapid and safe exploration of this discontinuous open zone over wide areas in search of food, as Crompton has argued (1984) for *Galago senegalensis*. But without the availability of readily acquired bulk, higher dependence upon arthropod prey has lead to greater behavioral specification than in *G. senegalensis*. The gracile lorisines, on the other hand, lacking any means of rapid locomotion, are limited to closed zones of the forest, and in this stratum foliage tangles provide such a closed, safer phase. Limitation to this very localized, restricted zone has lead, we would argue, to a more catholic choice of arthropod prey, including species such as hairy caterpillars and slugs neglected by other prosimians. Slow-climbing quadrupedalism is adequate for traveling this zone, since supports are densely packed.

A second set of external links for lorisines was "discovered" by both of our "control" visual groupers and the computer-produced dendrogram. This was a linkage of the two robust forms, again very distantly, with the lemurs and bushbabies. Thus, the large-bodied lorisines are closest externally to the bushbaby-mouse lemur group, in particular, the largest bodied of these, *Galago crassicaudatus*. There are resemblances in niche between *Perodicticus* and *G. crassicaudatus* (as, indeed, there are resemblances in anatomy). These are largely connected with a diet that includes substantial quantities of gums, even when in the dry and crystalline state.

It is not easy to suggest which of the two large-bodied lorisines are most closely linked with the gracile lorisines. In general, *Nycticebus* shows the greater similarity, if only because of a greater dependence upon animal foods. Similarly, the levels of resemblance of *Nycticebus* to *Perodicticus* on the one hand and to *Galago crassicaudatus* on the other are similar. Relatively frequent use of horizontal supports is actually more typical of the robust lorisines than of *G. crassicaudatus*, and both lorisines utilize climbing and slow quadrupedalism in place of leaping.

Large body size, use of horizontal supports, use of the canopy, and the eating of fruit seem to be related in some prosimians. This combination is the opposite of small body size, vertical supports, and an animal protein diet that seem to be associated in others. These seem to be two opposed strategies which in detail may contain several substrategies (see Crompton 1984).

Dietary constraints at large body size lead to frugivory. The concentration of fruit in the canopy in most tropical rain-forest trees leads to occupation of the high stratum. And an energetically poor, bulky diet encourages the use of the "arboreal motorways" represented by large, low-angled branches for lateral exploration.

Anatomies

The internal distances among the individual lorisines, especially the perceived extreme distance between the two subgroups, are nowhere near as great anatomically as appears here from consideration of lifestyles. Anatomical studies consistently find the two subgroups, and they also consistently place them together. The studies in question are those few morphometric investigations of Oxnard and colleagues that contain all four species. These include studies of the pelvic girdle and of overall limb proportions (Oxnard 1983). Given that we recognize the different scales of the two studies, the overall patterns of linkage are rather similar (fig. 5.15, compare with fig. 5.14).

Most of the factors that are responsible for this high degree of anatomical propinquity between the two lorisine groups are those to do with tensile forces acting in the limbs. Although we have documented the different ways in which this may occur in many species, we have not been able to separate out the special way in which it occurs in slow climbing (the predominant component for both groups of lorisines). In particular, we have not been able to include it at all in the quantitative diagrammatic profiles for each species. When it becomes possible to do this, then a closer link between the lifestyle profiles of the two groups of lorisines, although undoubtedly not of so great a degree as to disturb the two subgroups themselves, is likely to become apparent.

The relationships between the lifestyle profiles and the anatomical profiles for the external links of the lorisines with other species are less readily compared. The lifestyle information suggests that the external link is with *Galago crassicaudatus* (see fig. 5.14), but that species as a species was not available in the anatomical studies. According to the anatomical profiles (fig. 5.15), the closest link of the lorisines was indeed with the genus *Galago*. *Galago*, in this instance, means the mean position of all bushbabies studied (and this did include specimens of *G. crassicaudatus*. This external link, however, is through *Arctocebus* rather than *Perodicticus* as in the lifestyle profile.

As can readily be seen from the diagram of anatomical distances, the links

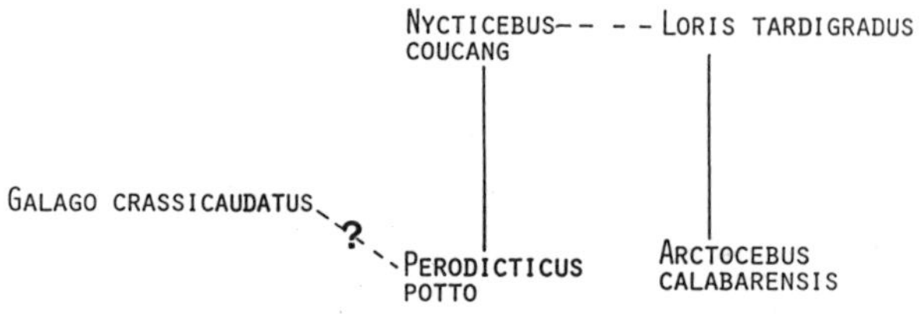

Fig. 5.14. The links implied by the relationships shown in figure 5.13 are displayed here.

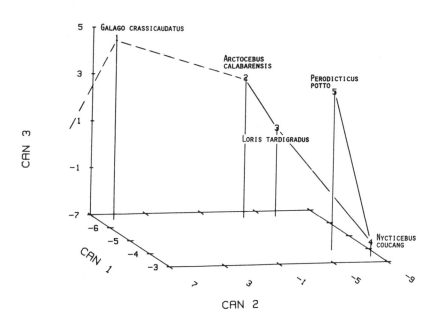

Fig. 5.15. The arrangement of the lorisines by a morphometric study of the pelvic girdle and femur. The plot shows a minimum spanning tree superimposed upon the model of relationships of the first three canonical axes.

between *Galago* and each of the other nearer lorisines are approximately equal. It seems likely that lack of functional information about tension in the lifestyle profiles (something that would render the two groups of lorisines far more similar if it were included), and the lack of anatomical information about species (anatomically they were dealt with at the coarser, generic, level), are responsible for the difference between the two types of investigation.

Our conclusion (despite missing data) must be that the detailed internal relationships and the overall external links of the two groups of lorisines determined from the study of lifestyles are similar to those of the two groups clearly evident in the study of anatomies. This is a level of association that was not achieved with the use of the older locomotor classifications and spectra.

Second Group: Cheirogaleines and Affines

Lifestyles

The cheirogaleines and most of the galagos are a well-defined group (figs. 5.16 and 5.17). This is more by reason of their locomotor totipotentiality than because of their specialization. One cheirogaleine, *Phaner*, is excluded from this group because it is (apart from its insect-secretion diet) a particularly unspecialized form that links well to both the indriids and lemurs. Two bushbabies, Allen's and Senegal, are also excluded because they are yet more highly specialized and link with other species (see below).

The locomotor profile of *Galago demidovii* resembles somewhat a bird in flight. The various cheirogaleine species depart more and more from this symmetrical shape through elongation of the "tail" and shortening of the "wings." The other bushbaby species depart from the "bird in flight" profile through the presentation of gradually increasing asymmetries of one kind or another. The overall differences are great enough that species at opposite sides of this complex circular group (e.g., the profiles for *Microcebus coquereli* and for *Galago elegantulus*) seem completely different. But the existence of the smaller discontinuities between neighboring profiles makes the entire set coherent.

The species within each of the two taxonomic groups do not seem to aggregate by taxon, with the exception perhaps of aggregation related to greater frequency of scurrying and greater consumption of animal items and fruit for the cheirogaleines, and with gummivory their major distinguishing feature.

Rather the two taxa pair-up in parallel specializations. The most obvious similarity is in the pairing of *Galago demidovii* with *Microcebus murinus*. Both species are adapted to life in foliage tangles, and range from canopy to undergrowth, with perhaps some preference for the former. Animal food is the predominant part of the diet, and small supports of any orientation are utilized. Unlike the similar niche of *Arctocebus* and *Loris tardigradus*, however, both species engage in similar amounts of saltation. They land from leaping, like all other members of the group, forefeet first. Climbing is used quite commonly, as indeed it is with the much more saltatory tarsiers. But perhaps most characteristic of both these forms is their scurrying locomotion, which is typically composed of short bursts of running interspersed with short leaps. Scurrying ignores support orientation as a major factor. This is what *Arctocebus* and *Loris* achieve in a much more limited (limiting) way with their mobile joints and elongated extremities. However, three- to four-limb support is inevitable in the latter case, while two-limb support is possible during running for *G. demidovii* and *M. murinus*. Stability and stealth, as a strategy for the fine-branch niche, is thus opposed to speed and surprise.

The other obvious pairing is between *Microcebus coquereli* and *Galago garnettii*. This rather straightforward comparison is a divergence of both spe-

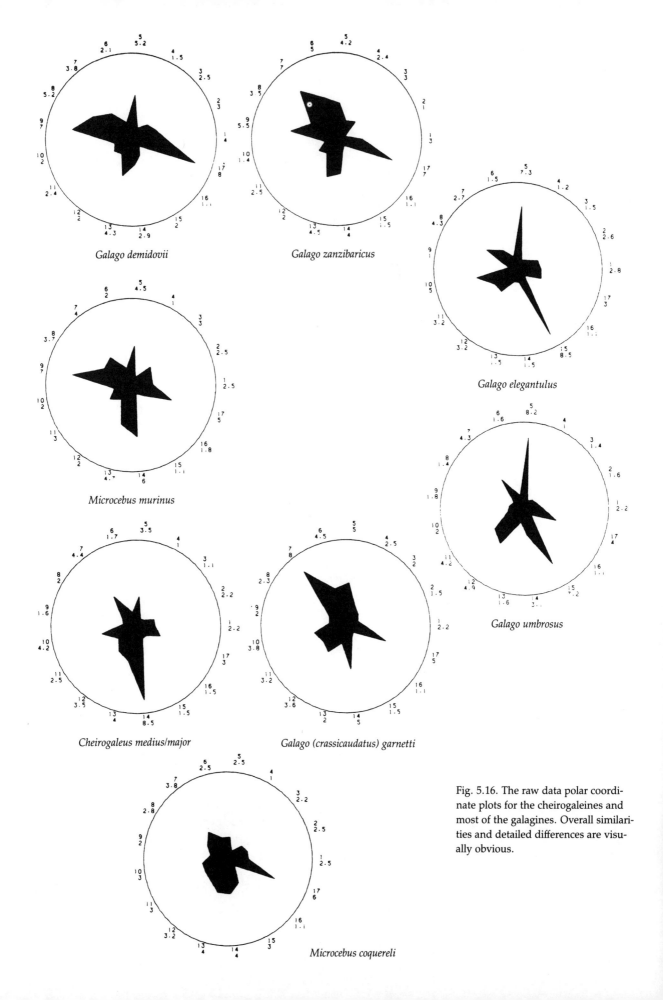

Galago demidovii

Galago zanzibaricus

Galago elegantulus

Microcebus murinus

Galago umbrosus

Cheirogaleus medius/major

Galago (crassicaudatus) garnetti

Fig. 5.16. The raw data polar coordinate plots for the cheirogaleines and most of the galagines. Overall similarities and detailed differences are visually obvious.

Microcebus coquereli

Fig. 5.17. The links implied by the relationships shown in figure 5.16 are displayed here.

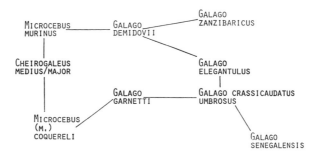

Fig. 5.18. The arrangement of the cheirogaleines and some of the galagines by a morphometric study of the pelvic girdle and femur. The plot shows a minimum spanning tree superimposed upon the model of relationships of the first three canonical axes.

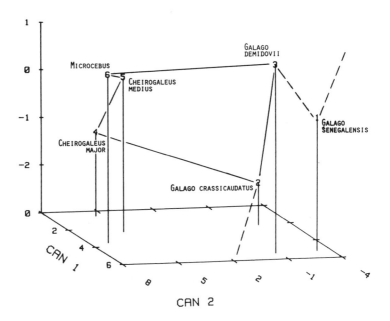

cies toward the typical genus-*Lemur* pattern: more fruit in the diet, and use of horizontal (often large) supports. This may stem from competition with the genus *Lemur* for *M. coquereli*, and perhaps with monkeys for *G. garnettii*. Neither form has become canopy-living, and both utilize frequent saltation as well as quadrupedal locomotion. *Cheirogaleus medius* and *major* are both considerably more dependent upon fruit. The latter two species, which still take a considerable (or greater) quantity of arthropod prey, show more affinity to horizontal, large branches.

Of the galagines, *Galago zanzibaricus* is rather similar to *G. demidovii*, with small dietary shifts in emphasis away from arthropod prey and toward fruit and gums. It is more restricted to the undergrowth than *G. demidovii*, and its locomotion is possibly more specialized toward leaping. Data are insufficient for a complete analysis.

We detect a continuum between the remaining two galagos, *Galago elegantulus* and *G. crassicaudatus*, in the direction of greater niche specialization. They tend toward larger body size and gummivory. Their level of gummivory may be a response to sympatric competitors—for *G. elegantulus* by the presence of *Perodicticus*, and for *G. crassicaudatus* by the presence of *G. se-*

negalensis. Thus, *G. elegantulus* has specialized toward the acquisition of droplet gum sources on large vertical supports, and *G. crassicaudatus* toward a somewhat potto-like adaptation within the behavioral and anatomical constraints of being a galago.

The cheirogaleines and most of the galagos thus possibly represent (behaviorally) two phylogenetically related groups whose members demonstrate a parallel adaptive radiation, filling similar niches in similar ways.

Anatomies

It is, again, not so immediately obvious what the relationships are between the patterns of grouping revealed by the above studies of lifestyles and those given by the anatomical investigations that have already been carried out. The anatomical studies are the morphometric investigations of the pelvic girdle and femur and overall limb proportions that are summarized in Oxnard (1983). The reasons for the difficulties are the same as before. The prior morphometric investigations were not aimed at so fine a level of distinction as that between species. And several species are missing in the anatomical studies. However, enough of the same species are present in both studies that some alliances are apparent between them.

The entire group (fig. 5.18) approximates a circular arrangement similar to that evident from the profiles of lifestyles (compare figs. 5.17 and 5.18). The cheirogaleines lie at one side of this arrangement, the bushbabies at the other, in both studies.

The external links of this circular group are also quite similar in the two investigations. One is a link with *Galago senegalensis*, a member of the tarsiers and affines; the other is a link with the lorisines (but with *Arctocebus* rather than *Perodicticus*) as in the profile of lifestyles.

Third Group: Tarsiers and Affines

Lifestyles

The three tarsiers form a distinctive profile (figs. 5.19 and 5.20) resulting from their almost exclusively animal diet and their remarkable affinity for vertical supports. To an extent that is yet uncertain, all tarsiers utilize the undergrowth in preference to any other zone. Lack of systematic study of freeranging tarsiers prevents any reliable estimate of the frequency of use of this stratum. Limited reports of *Tarsius syrichta*, combined with the poverty of the Philippines forest, have encouraged a very high estimate of the frequency of use of the "tree trunk and ground zone" by *T. syrichta*, greater than for *T. bancanus* and *T. spectrum*. Estimates for stratum preferences for the latter two are based upon the McKinnons' preliminary report of *T. spectrum* and the more extensive work by Niemitz on *T. bancanus*. Reports for *T. bancanus* are conflicting and we have adopted a conservative (and probably underestimated) figure for stratum preference. Locomotion is dominated in

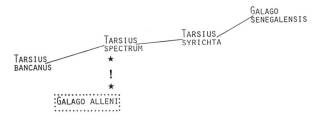

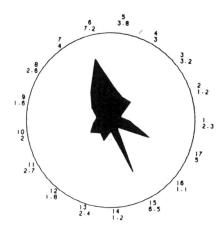

Galago senegalensis

Fig. 5.19. The links implied by the relationships shown in figure 5.20 are displayed here.

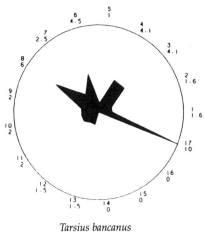

Tarsius bancanus

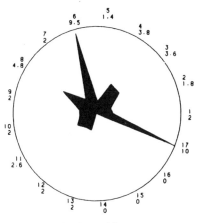

Tarsius syrichta

Fig. 5.20. This figure displays the raw data polar coordinate plots for the tarsiers and their neighboring bushbabies. Overall similarities and detailed differences are visually obvious. The small inset for *Galago alleni* shows the plot as modified by the work of Redford et al. 1984; see comments on pages 140–41.

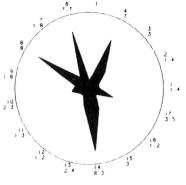

Galago alleni

all three by ricochetal and crouching leaps (but these are certainly not to the exclusion of climbing), and some quadrupedalism. The exclusivity of leaping in tarsiers may be exaggerated because of the paucity of cage environments in which they have been observed. It is certainly more frequent, however, than in any other small prosimian.

The most obvious comparisons can be made outside this coherent grouping with *Galago senegalensis* and *G. alleni*, though, as is readily evident from their profiles, these comparisons are not especially close. *G. senegalensis* is more distinct in terms of stratum and support use (venturing more often into the canopy, but encountering vertical supports less frequently, possibly as a consequence of its common utilization of gums in the diet) than for any marked difference in locomotion. However, it probably does leap less than *G. alleni*, and uses running leaps and falling leaps more than do tarsiers.

In addition, but as with *Galago alleni*, the typical crouching and ricochetal leaps of *G. senegalensis* are quite unlike those of any other small prosimians with the exception of tarsiers. Leaps are made with the body in a vertical position, and with the hindlimbs landing first, being retracted immediately after take-off. In *G. senegalensis* the locomotor features, specialized leaps, hopping, and relative affinity for vertical body postures allow safe and rapid exploration of a wide area of the ground for arthropod prey. The environment features fit with this, vertical tree and sapling trunks serving as vantage points to survey the ground for prey and to which to escape.

No doubt the very similar ricochetal and leaping behavior of the tarsier is an adaptation to a similar habitat, although the specialization of locomotion is more extreme in tarsiers, just as diet is more specialized and potential food sources more limited.

Galago alleni is even more problematical. Charles-Dominique describes the species in such a way that its degree of specialization resembles that of the tarsiers more than of *G. senegalensis*, even though *G. alleni*'s leaping seems a little less stylized and its anatomy more generalized. The stylized hindlimb-first landing leap of the tarsiers and *G. senegalensis* is probably an adaptation to movement between well-separated supports of medium to large size, and possibly specifically to vertical supports. The reason for the less stylized forelimb-first landing of *G. alleni* is difficult to explain at this stage, because we lack a quantitative field report to confirm Charles-Dominique's findings. Presumably, specific biomechanical characteristics of the leap of *G. alleni*—such as velocity, typical distance, and characteristics of the initial support—contrast with those of *G. senegalenis* and the tarsiers.

We think it possible that the large fruit element posited as existing for the diet of *Galago alleni* is incorrect. It may actually represent the consumption of invertebrates that are attracted to rotting fruit on the ground (see Redford et al. 1984). This would fit much closer with a tarsier-like habitus, as *Tarsius bancanus* is frequently attracted to rotting fruit (Fogden 1974, and personal communication from the Sabah Forest Department staff). If this is indeed true, then a modification would be required in the profile for *G. alleni*. This is shown in the reduced inset in figure 5.20, though, of course, we have not yet used it in the clustering processes.

The functional mechanism involved in leaping in tarsiers, *Galago alleni*, and *G. senegalensis* seems distinct from those of the lemurines and indriids. In particular, elongation and development of rotation in the tarsus characterizes the tarsiers and galagos but not the lemurines and indriids. A separate derivation of the two groups of hindlimb-first landing leapers seems likely. This is underlined by several, possibly "primitive," characteristics of tarsier locomotion which have not been replaced by leaping, such as frequency of scurrying behavior. It is "primitive," of course, only if one assumes that Charles-Dominique's and Martin's characterization of *Galago demidovii/Microcebus*-like anatomy and behavioral pattern for the ancestral stock of primates of modern aspect is correct.

Anatomies

It is, once again, somewhat difficult to make direct comparisons with prior anatomical (morphometric) studies. But results are available for the aforementioned investigations of the hip and thigh, and overall limb proportions (Oxnard 1983). In those investigations, tarsiers are only represented by the mean for the genus. Nevertheless, Allen's and Senegal bushbabies are separately represented, as are several other outlying species that are present in the lifestyles studies. The tarsiers and the two extreme bushbabies do link together as a group (fig. 5.21) and to this degree certainly resemble the grouping derived from the study of lifestyles (compare with fig. 5.20).

The external link of this group with other prosimians is from *Galago senegalensis* to precisely the same two galagine species as in the clustering based upon lifestyle data: *G. elegantulus* and *G. demidovii* (given that the intermediate *G. crassicaudatus* is missing from the anatomical [morphometric] studies, fig. 5.21). Thus the association between lifestyles and anatomies is almost perfect for these prosimians.

Fig. 5.21. The arrangement of the tarsiers and their neighboring bushbabies by a morphometric study of the pelvic girdle and femur. The plot shows a minimum spanning tree superimposed upon the model of relationships of the first three canonical axes.

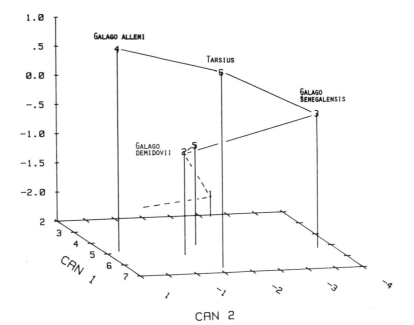

Fourth Group: Indriids and Affines

Lifestyles

The indriids present a united but graded group of specialized leapers, which are linked externally and internally with nonindriids (figs. 5.22 and 5.23). The overall profile for *Indri* has the shape of a butterfly with "spikes."

The spikes of the indriid plots are due to the dependence of the diet of many indriids on leaves and buds and on fruit, together with zero values for the neighboring characteristics. The two "wings" are produced by their habitat (a preference for large supports, frequently vertical) and by their leaping (especially ricochetal leaping which characterizes all of the group). The stratum is less well-defined, but the canopy is often used.

Hapalemur, the grey gentle lemur, as we have observed, is indri-like in behavior in association with the very limited variety of supports available for locomotion in its reed-bed and bamboo-grove habitats. Its leaping behavior is by no means as specialized as that of the indriids. *Hapalemur* itself links with *Lemur catta* in the group of *Lemur* and its affines. Most of these species combine a relatively high degree of ricochetal leaping (but unlike indriids, not crouching leaping) with some considerable affinity for utilizing vertical supports near ground level. However, *Hapalemur* justifiably falls with the indriids rather than with the lemur group, as its propensity for vertical clinging surpasses any performances regularly observed in *L. catta.*

Lepilemur is unquestionably a member of this group, as a specialist folivore with strong affinity for vertical supports of large diameter. Like *Hapalemur,* though, its behavior may be strongly conditioned by the very limited support choice in the Didiereaceae forest where it has been observed. For example, on the ground it walks or, if forced, hops bipedally, or leaps, but differently from the specialized bipedal hopping of *Propithecus* or the ricochetal leaping of *Indri* when at ground level. Its crouching leaps, however, are of the indriid type.

We have observed above that the behavior of *Propithecus* is quite labile, and it links externally with *Phaner* largely on the basis of this totipotentiality. The indriids are by no means as isolated and unique a group in terms of locomotor behavior as the tarsiers. Rather, one could almost describe them as at the opposite end of a lemuriform "functional spectrum" to the quadrupedal, branch-running lemurs such as *Lemur fulvus.* This is indeed the meaning of the indriid "ray" proceeding from centrally aligned lemurs in the star-shaped functional and anatomical spectra of Oxnard (1983).

Leaf-eating appears to us to provide the key to this. Both *Hapalemur* and *Lepilemur,* with a leaf or shoot diet, have adopted *Indri*-like behavior. Clearly, an animal does not have to be specialized to eat leaves, as Pollock (1979) points out, but it often helps. *Alouatta,* for instance, has become quite specialized in a not entirely different direction. Suspension may be part of

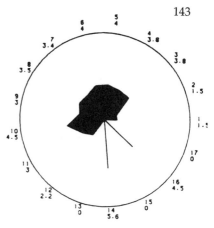

Propithecus verreauxi

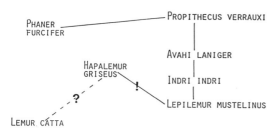

Fig. 5.22. The links implied by the relationships shown in figure 5.23 are displayed here.

Fig. 5.23. This figure displays the raw data polar coordinate plots for the indriids and affines. Overall similarities and detailed differences are visually obvious.

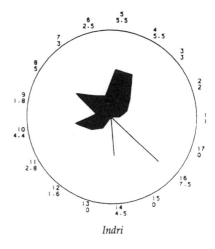

Indri

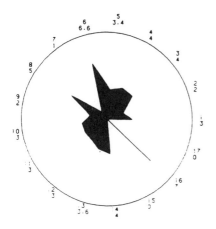

Hapalemur griseus

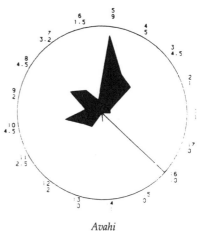

Avahi

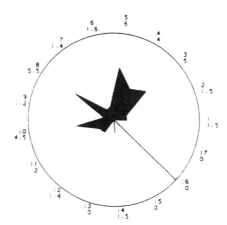

Lepilemur mustelinus

the answer for the large-bodied indriids; classically large-bodied forms need suspension to stabilize themselves in the canopy. But for *Lepilemur* and *Hapalemur*, large body-size/suspension relationships will not provide the answer, as neither engages in suspensory behavior to anything like the degree that occurs in indriids. It is, perhaps, adaptation to the extremes, together with prior vertical clinging and ricochetal leaping/hopping propensities (perhaps derived from a *Lemur catta*-like ancestor) that have molded indriid behavior, and so with *Lepilemur* and *Hapalemur*. For *Lepilemur* and *Propithecus*, there is the unique structure of the Didiereaceae forest, with possible energetic constraints that put a premium on fast lateral movement—predator threats cannot, surely, be a pressure in Madagascar—which for folivores would probably mean small patch size and large interpatch distance.

For *Indri* in its lush, wet mixed forest the solution may be more obscure. It is possible that movement directly between tree trunks may be conditioned by the necessity of eating earth daily because of an incomplete supply of minerals from leaves or fruit. This may necessitate a move down to the undergrowth, where discontinuity urges saltation. The analogy may rather be with *Pongo*. Large body size may lead not only to suspension but to a new strategy for harvesting fruit and leaves: bring food rather than go where the food is, as its smaller lemurine competitors can do.

If, as it appears, *Indri* is highly limited in the type of leaves that it can eat, then patch size and interpatch distance again are another pressure toward saltation below the continuous canopy rather than necessarily slow quadrupedal movement within it.

Unquestionably, more knowledge of ecology is needed before these problems can be solved.

Fig. 5.24. The arrangement of the indriids and affines by a morphometric study of the pelvic girdle and femur. The plot shows a minimum spanning tree superimposed upon the model of relationships of the first three canonical axes.

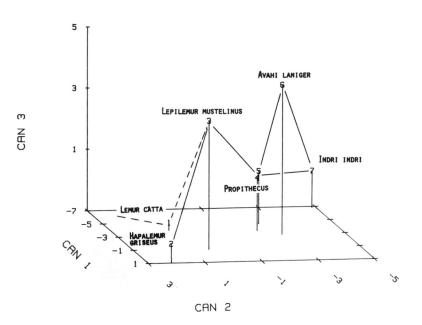

Anatomies

In the case of this group, totally comparable anatomical (morphometric) studies exist because precisely these same groups have been examined together for the hip and thigh and for overall limb proportions (Oxnard 1983).

The morphometric results (fig. 5.24) for the internal arrangements of the group are almost identical with those stemming from the study of lifestyles (fig. 5.23). These same results are only a little less similar from the point of view of external links, and as to whether or not *Hapalemur* should be directly (lifestyles) or only secondarily (anatomies) linked to the group.

Overall, there is a truly remarkable concordance between the multidimensional assessments of lifestyles and the multidimensional analyses of anatomies in this group.

Fifth Group: Lemurs, Daubentonia, and Phaner

Lifestyles

The lemurs (figs. 5.25 and 5.26) do not represent as unified a picture as the previously described groups (fig. 5.22). Their profiles, overall, are more disparate. Nevertheless, although outlying members seem rather different from one another, as individual neighboring members are compared with one another, the patterns among them vary less and outline a regular spectrum of difference.

Varecia and *Lemur fulvus,* despite our very limited knowledge of *Varecia,* appear to be similar: having a fruit diet, quite frequently using horizontal supports, moving predominantly by climbing or slow quadrupedalism, and using leaps mainly to fill in the gaps between branches or to make shortcuts en route in the canopy. They differ in the greater specialization of *L. fulvus* toward life in the continuous, closed canopy, where they seem to avoid moving off continuous routes along horizontal branches. *Varecia* seems more labile in its behavior, including using a greater degree of suspension as befits its body size, and venturing into the undergrowth. *L. catta* is unquestionably adapted further in this direction, but its lability of behavior, including the ability to move by saltation between major angled or vertical branches, has presumably contributed to its greater success. It may well be indicating the direction in which ancestral indriids moved in separating from lemurids.

Lemur mongoz is separated from the "generalized" lemur in a different direction. It is specialized toward the use of large horizontal supports, but it is somewhat more saltatory than *L. fulvus.* Perhaps these modifications reflect the additional demands on extensive lateral exploration suggested by its rather specialized diet, which centers on nectar-bearing flowers.

Finally, *Daubentonia,* with a yet more specialized diet heavily dependent

Fig. 5.25. The links implied by the relationships shown in figure 5.26 are displayed here.

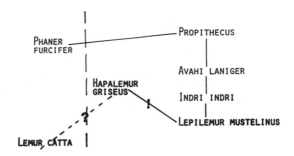

upon grubs as well as fruit, is also relatively saltatory, but in its need to search for large (old, and hence more often insect-invaded) branches, has diverged in a direction that recalls *Galago crassicaudatus* or *G. elegantulus*, involving frequent climbing and suspensory postures.

Thus, the lemurs present one particular lifestyle—a canopy, fruit, horizontal branch, slow quadrupedalism niche—from which particular species are separated in different adaptive directions that recall, but do not equal, the more extreme specializations of other prosimian groups.

Phaner is included with the lemurs only because it is a generalist with attachments to several other groups, and it has been discussed separately above. An almost equal argument could be made for its closer association with the other cheirogaleines. But, of all the cheirogaleines, it is the one that bears most comparison with outside groupings.

Anatomies

We are able to present an association between these lifestyle groupings and anatomical (morphometric) groups based upon the studies of the hip and thigh and overall limb proportions (Oxnard 1983). It is, once again, a limited comparison because of the reduced numbers of groups in the morphometric analysis as compared with the lifestyle studies (cf. fig. 5.27 and fig. 5.25).

The same main group—all lemurs—is defined. But its internal relationships are not especially similar in the two studies. In part, this is because not all species are available for each. But it is also partly because the anatomical distances between the species of *Lemur*, as can be seen from the shortness of the links in the figure, are so small that they are almost all the same. This means that no particular dendrogram is statistically much more likely than any other. With such small distances, many minor perturbations, for instance due to biological variation within the samples available, are likely to be all that account for the particular form the dendrogram has taken. That the lemurs fall together anatomically as well as in terms of lifestyles, is, however, not at all in doubt.

In addition to links with *Lemur* species, the other internal link in the present ecological study is with *Daubentonia*. The anatomical studies show that there is indeed a link between lemurs and *Daubentonia*. But they place *Dau-*

Fig. 5.26. This figure displays the raw data polar coordinate plots for the lemurs and affines. Overall similarities and detailed differences are visually obvious.

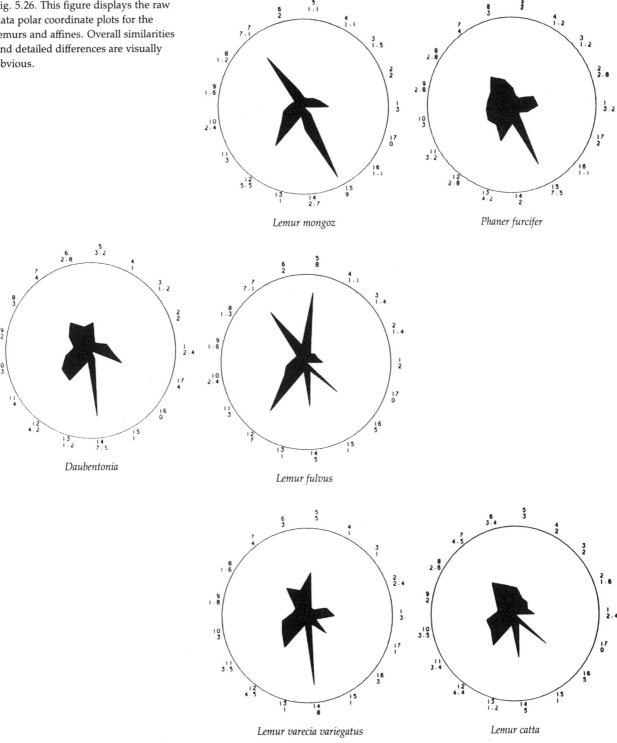

Lemur mongoz

Phaner furcifer

Daubentonia

Lemur fulvus

Lemur varecia variegatus

Lemur catta

Fig. 5.27. The arrangement of the
lemurs and affines by a morphometric
study of the pelvic girdle and femur.
The plot shows a minimum spanning
tree superimposed upon the model of
relationships of the first three canonical
axes.

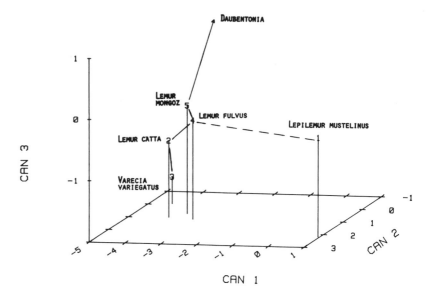

bentonia so distantly that it is really a total outlier (the continuous line going
off the plot in figure 5.27) to all prosimians. Its position anatomically is
figured in detail in Oxnard (1981). In both studies, however, this species
does have its closest link with prosimians through the true lemurs. The
anatomical studies are so extensive that it cannot be doubted that this great
difference is real. It has not been possible to carry out the lifestyle studies
in such a way as to emphasize those features peculiar to *Daubentonia,* and
their habits of leaping, diet, foraging, and so on, have not been properly
recorded in our profiles. It is possible that if this information had been included, *Daubentonia* would appear as outlying in lifestyle as in anatomy.

The external anatomical links of the group also differ from the lifestyle
information. Figure 5.27 shows the primary external link of the true lemurs
to be from *Lemur fulvus* to *Hapalemur.* A second link is between *Lemur catta*
and *Lepilemur.* This fits in principle, though not in detail, with the anatomical results. *Phaner* is absent in the anatomical studies so that presence or
absence of that link cannot be examined. *Hapalemur* is present in the anatomical studies, but the actual link in those studies between lemurs and
affines and indriids and affines is with *Lepilemur. Hapalemur* is, however, the
next nearest species to the lemurs and might well, given slightly different
expressions of biological variability, actually be the nearest species.

It is only in the case of this last group, therefore, that the associations
between lifestyles and anatomies are not overly close. Almost certainly this
is merely because (a) too many species are missing from the anatomical
investigations, and (b) too much lifestyle information is missing for *Daubentonia* and possibly others.

6 Prosimian Lifestyles and Anatomies in Summary

We have set out in this book to present a method for the summary and comparison of primate locomotor activities, habitat utilizations, and dietary preferences that produce reasonably objective, readily comparable, and easily replicable and testable descriptions. These are descriptions that encompass a fairly large part of the multidimensional context of locomotion.

We have discussed the defects of past attempts to impose classificatory order on primate locomotor behavior. First, global categories such as "quadruped" and "vertical clinger and leaper" imply similarity in activities that are actually quite distinct. Since much of the effort of studies of primate locomotor behavior has been directed at interpreting the functional and evolutionary significance of morphological differences between species, such confusion of functional systems is undesirable.

Second, locomotor activities can be only artificially viewed as entities distinct from their natural context, such as the supports upon which they are performed and the foods that they help to garner. Moreover, they form a part of many other daily activities such as playing and escaping, and they are, in part, under the same selective pressures as these other activities. Several recent studies have demonstrated the quantitative relations between locomotor activities and anatomy that exist even at the species-group level (summarized in Oxnard 1983). Indeed, some studies have gone further and demonstrated the manner in which differences in locomotor activities between individual species are related to differences in niche and in particular foraging strategies.

These demonstrations cannot, of themselves, produce reliable generalizations about the adaptive role of locomotor activity. The relationships need to be shown repeatedly, for valid generalizations to be established. Accordingly, our review of prosimian locomotor behavior has attempted to retain the multidimensionality of action in the natural context, while presenting quantitative data in a readily assimilable form that reasonably easily allows multiple comparisons of species profiles.

We have recognized that the process of extracting quantified "scores" for the lifestyle variables from verbal descriptions is fraught with difficulties, but we see no other alternative as long as so few objective data are available. Further, we have recognized that, at present, our approach has not encompassed local variability in behavior (for most species we can only sign our recognition of the importance of local differences by noting whether data were obtained from captive or freeranging populations, and if the latter, from which sites). These methods could even be applied to local populations of individual species, should appropriate lifestyle and anatomical data ever become available.

Our selection of variables has been as objective, yet realistic, as we could make it. There is no information available to us that we have excluded. The selection has been based upon our knowledge and experience, and on assessment of the possible biomechanical or other significance of particular behaviors. The lists of variables will have to be amended as our knowledge grows, and the species groups may change accordingly. Further, the present approach cannot replace detailed individual or species-group study, which shows the precise relationship of locomotor and other aspects of the lifestyle, and which alone can assess the adaptive role of lifestyles, as well as their frequency in particular behavioral contexts. And finally, this approach stresses the *frequent* behavior rather than the peak-load inducing behavior or the uncommon but adaptively crucial behavior. We must find ways of including these latter data.

Groupings of Activity, Environment, and Diet

Our results have been obtained, in the first instance, from plots of raw scores for all variables along polar coordinates, the length of each radius representing relative frequency or relative score for each variable. Our results have been confirmed by second-order multivariate analyses of the raw data, although full description of these results awaits publication in the primary scientific literature.

The star-shaped plots provide a readily assimilable summary of the lifestyle data for each species. In particular, comparisons between plots are readily made, allowing recognition of strongly similar species, distinction of unique species, and arrangement of species into lifestyle spectra. Each of these were distinguished in the present first-order visualization. They provide a useful method of displaying locomotor activities, habitat utilizations, and dietary preferences, both separately and as a multidimensional mosaic. They were preserved and further explicated in the second-order multivariate statistical analyses.

The data show only a moderate tendency to group by taxon but the presence of any such tendency indicates the influence of phylogeny on behavior. Typically, most members of a taxon were found not far from each other. But single or multiple linkages with individual species of other taxa arrange them linearly or circularly rather than as isolated clusters. Interpretation of such linear and circular arrangements are usually most readily made in terms of niche spectra, with individual species at varying positions within them.

Plots for some individual species were found to fit best outside the clusterings or spectra of their own taxon. In some cases this could most readily be interpreted as indicating their "totipotentiality" or generalized locomotor repertoire, as was the case with *Phaner*. In other cases the accounts of their lifestyles fit much better interpretations speaking to specializations outside their own taxon, as was the case with *Galago alleni*.

Five major groupings were distinguished.

1. lorisines
2. cheirogaleines (excluding *Phaner*) and galagines (excluding *Galago alleni* and *G. senegalensis*)
3. tarsiers, together with the latter two *Galago* species
4. indriids, with *Lepilemur* and *Hapalemur*
5. lemurines, together with *Daubentonia* and *Phaner*

The lorisines are perhaps not to be considered as a coherent lifestyle grouping on the basis of present information; they clearly are a coherent group anatomically and morphometrically (fig. 6.1).

When additional information becomes available about tension-bearing in its different forms, the combining of the lorisines into a single lifestyle

Fig. 6.1. Comparison of the lifestyle and anatomical arrangements of the species in group 1: the lorisines.

Lifestyles: Niche metrics

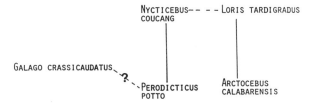

Anatomies: Morphometrics

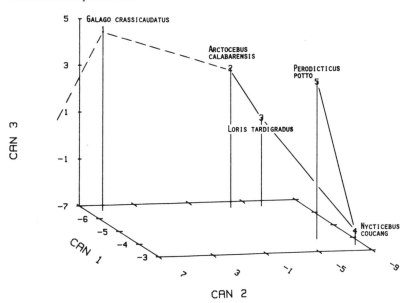

grouping may be more evident. They currently form two pairs whose major common feature is the *absence* of leaping. Our results echo McArdle's observation (1981) that there are two distinct anatomical types, a gracile and a robust, each with an African and an Asian representative. The two pairs differ most markedly in the preference of the gracile pair for undergrowth, small supports, and a more wholly animal-food diet.

The relative frequency of climbing and use of supports in different orientations does not as readily distinguish the two pairs, intra-pair differences being equal to or larger than inter-pair differences. We have suggested that the gracile forms inhabit a closed phase of the undergrowth, as do, partially, *Microcebus* and *Galago demidovii*. But, though the rapid saltatory locomotion of the latter may allow use equally of such fine branch tangles in the undergrowth and canopy (and perhaps easier interpatch travel), the purely quadrumanual locomotion of the lorisines has limited them to a small lateral and vertical range in the undergrowth. This, in turn, may have demanded a more catholic diet and low-energy budget leading to further locomotor specializations and further uniqueness.

Plots for the robust pair of lorisines, however, link externally with *Galago crassicaudatus*. The features that are common to these two are high-bulk (gum or fruit) diet, use of the canopy, preference for supports of low angle, some preference for large supports and common climbing, and (to a lesser extent) slow quadrupedalism. *Nycticebus* and *G. crassicaudatus* in particular use slow quadrupedalism frequently. Although not noted among our variables (as in prosimians, it is never a *very common* activity), suspensory locomotion and postural suspension are again typical of the two robust lorisines and *G. crassicaudatus*, which are largest in body size in the Lorisidae. Thus, we have observed that a heavily gummivorous diet in *Perodicticus* and *G. crassicaudatus* implies the need for large body size and low-energy investment in locomotion. Suspension is of particular relevance to access major gum sources underneath major branches or on tree trunks. Structural characteristics of gum-bearing African trees such as the acacias and of the trees of the Sinomalayan tropical forest are likely to be relevant to an understanding of locomotion of all three species. This relates especially to the most continuous lateral paths that are on horizontal or near horizontal branches in the closed canopy. However, *G. crassicaudatus'* locomotion, being partly saltatory, is more closely related to that of its congeners than to the lorisines, although it lies in the direction of the lorisine position.

The cheirogaleines and the galagines have a common locomotor versatility, with quadrupedalism, saltatory locomotion, and scurrying as some of the shared locomotor elements; they also share many anatomical features (fig. 6.2).

They tend to differ by taxon in a greater concentration on fruit and animal items and more frequent scurrying locomotion in the cheirogaleines versus the innovation of gummivory and lesser scurrying in the galagines. There are not consistent differences in saltatory or other quadrupedal locomotion,

Fig. 6.2. Comparison of the lifestyle and anatomical arrangements of the species in group 2: the cheirogaleines and some galagines.

Lifestyles: Niche Metrics

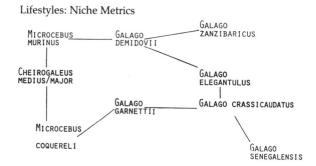

Anatomies: Morphometrics

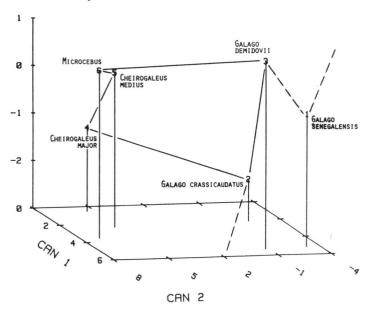

nor in support usages. Rather, as we have noted, specific pairs—*Microcebus murinus* and *Galago demidovii*, and *M. coquereli* and *G. garnettii*—may have radiated from common unspecialized stocks in adaptive (including locomotor) parallelism. This may or may not reflect the influence of recent and common phylogenetic relationships. Gummivory in the galagines, partly responsible no doubt for their greater evolutionary success, does not precisely determine their locomotor behavior. It is less a single adaptive strategy than a set of alternative related strategies, depending upon body size, and relative exclusiveness and specialization in droplet or "gum-lick" (localized gum concentration) feeding.

Galago elegantulus' and *G. crassicaudatus'* plots are similar up to a point, but small body size, relatively common saltation, and preference for vertical supports are contrasted with large body size, relatively common climbing, slow quadrupedalism, and some preference for horizontal supports in the two species, both of which are largely canopy dwellers.

Gummivory as a primary dietary choice seems less generally consistent with preference for the undergrowth: compare the plot for *Galago senegalensis*. Here animal items are considerably more important. In the predominance of crouching or ricochetal leaping locomotion, if less than in an increased preference for vertical supports, *G. senegalensis* seems to resemble the tarsiers. It also comes to lie centrally in our groupings together with *Phaner:* the commonalities being both locomotor versatility and considerable dependency on saps (*Phaner*) or gums (*G. senegalensis*). Indeed, it seems that saps and gums as a major dietary element almost always lead to locomotor versatility. *Phaner's* saltatory locomotion, however, has probably been overstressed in the literature and its position here is therefore likely to be changed as we come to know more. In detail, *Phaner's* leaping is essentially of the cheirogaleine type (scurrying and running and falling leaps, into forelimb-first landings) and quite unlike that of *G. senegalensis, Propithecus,* and the tarsiers, which are all, to some extent, more specialized and biomechanically similar in their saltation. The emphasis on frequency is certainly a weakness in the present study.

Both in frequency and in biomechanics the saltatory locomotion of *Galago senegalensis* and the tarsiers is quite clearly distinct among the prosimians; anatomically these species are also quite distinct (fig. 6.3). Although intriguing biomechanical distinctions remain to be elucidated (such as the function of the ankle joint), the frequency of leaping (over 50 percent in tarsiers and *Galago senegalensis*) and its generally stylized form allies *G. senegalensis* firmly with tarsiers. Leaping in *G. demidovii* is common (40 percent) but typical of that of the cheirogaleine, galago group, with horizontal body posture and forelimb-first landing. No doubt, too, the ecological role of the leaping locomotion is very similar, as we have observed above. Stratum and use of supports, are, however, contrasted in the much greater specialization of the tarsiers to the "low zone" and the use of vertical supports.

Galago alleni's position in this grouping must remain somewhat equivocal until we have confirmation of Charles-Dominique's intriguing field report. Biomechanically, its leaping contrasts too much with that of *G. senegalensis* or the tarsiers, as does its frugivory, for its lifestyle to be so readily linked with them. However, the frugivory, as we have suggested, may not be all that it appears. If this proves correct, then the firm links among an animal diet, use of undergrowth, and ricochetal and crouching saltatory locomotion would be even further enhanced, and would be one of the more striking results of this study.

The indriids and their behavioral affines are an intriguing contrast. Their leaping locomotion and their use of vertical supports provide a third example of such specialized locomotion among the Prosimii. Anatomically also, they demonstrate a fourth grouping (fig. 6.4).

Diet, stratum, and support-size preference are quite distinct (excluding

Fig. 6.3. Comparison of the lifestyle and anatomical arrangements of the species in group 3: the tarsiers and two galagines.

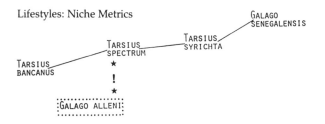

Lifestyles: Niche Metrics

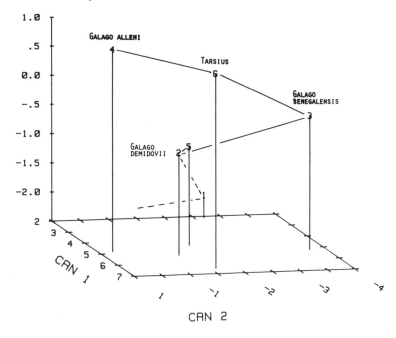

Anatomies: Morphometrics

Hapalemur for a moment), and the leaping style is, as we have noted, different again. Body postures during the leap are variable, and forelimb involvement in landing and in support while clinging to verticals is much more significant.

We suspect that the relationship between energy budgets, foraging strategies, and locomotor activities are similar to those of the tarsier/galago group. Saltatory locomotion in the indriids is, we suspect, as much adaptive to wide dispersal of food sites and high (here, total, not relative) energy costs of locomotion, as it is likely to be in both the tarsiers and *Galago senegalensis*. The open tree trunk zone just below the closed canopy obviously offers a similar structure to the near ground zone, in its vertical supports and discontinuity.

Neither is support size (relative to body size) markedly different. It is the *Microcebus/Galago demidovii* group of specialist leapers and vertical support users which is distinct in this, preferring relatively small supports.

Fig. 6.4. Comparison of the lifestyle
and anatomical arrangements of the
species in group 4: the indriids, with
Lepilemur and *Hapalemur*.

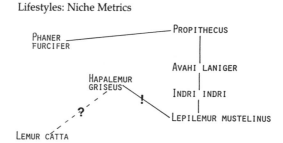

Lifestyles: Niche Metrics

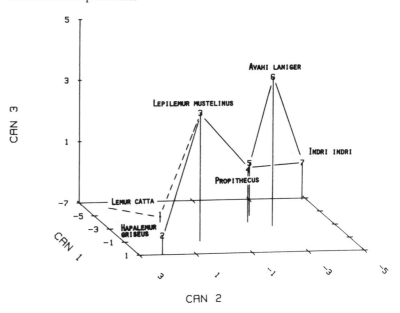

Anatomies: Morphometrics

The parallels, however, are not exact. The indriids are presumably searching the canopy above, not the ground below, for food. Walking, if it occurs,
happens therefore on branches in the periphery of the trees, not on the
ground, and probably occurs in a similar context of "detailed foraging" (i.e.,
searching the immediate area for individual food items).

Lepilemur is behaviorally an indriid (in locomotion at least) but with reservations that indicate lemurid ancestry in its more generalized locomotor
behavior when moving on the ground. *Hapalemur*, we feel, is an example of
extreme behavioral constraints imposed by support availability. Its locomotor capabilities are much more generalized than those of the indriids or
Lepilemur. Most certainly, however, it must be at least anatomically and behaviorally predisposed to vertical clinging postures to choose the very odd
habitat it has selected. Certainly it is a very indriid-like lemur, even in its
leaping style. However, it is distinct in its lack of forelimb suspensory behavior, even in its vertical clinging; and in the few leaps we have examined,

Fig. 6.5. Comparison of the lifestyle and anatomical arrangements of the species in group 5: the lemurines, with *Daubentonia* and *Phaner*.

Lifestyles: Niche Metrics

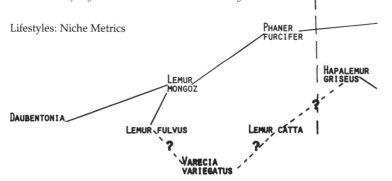

Anatomies: Morphometrics

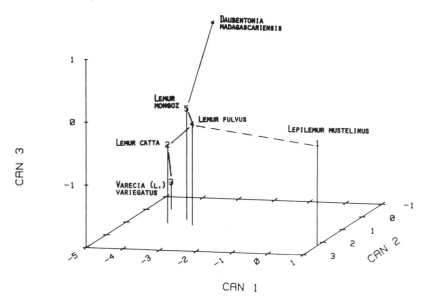

it does not adopt the high forelimb posture that indriids so frequently use.

The roots of forelimb suspension in the indriids, as indeed the roots of their saltatory locomotion, are surely set with the indri-like lemurs. The lemurid lemurs exhibit a graded spectrum of locomotor adaptation. This ranges from the very versatile *Lemur catta*, which we suspect in a more "vertical habitat" would look quite indriid-like, to the slow quadrupedal specialism of *L. fulvus*.

Only a moderately coherent profile of behaviors, but a markedly coherent pattern of anatomies, was noted for the lemurines (fig. 6.5). They show a combination of preference for horizontal supports of large diameter, slow quadrupedalism, use of the canopy, and frugivory. Cheirogaleines (and perhaps *Galago garnettii* among the galagines) seem to have a similar adaptive pattern, but here located in the middle story of the forest.

Finally, it is possible to compare the profile of lifestyles of all species taken together, with the profile of anatomies that they display. In this case there is only a moderate association between the two profiles. In the main, this is because the suite of animal groups in the studies of anatomy were somewhat more restricted and mainly at the generic level. Nevertheless, the degree of association that exists is remarkably good (fig. 6.6).

We have also learned from this analysis about the relationships existing among habitat and locomotor variables. Diet seems to express itself less often directly than indirectly, through patch size and patch dispersion, and through energetic relationship. Frugivory does not itself lead to a particular kind of locomotion, and neither does carnivory. The two terms are too coarse.

Stratum is not a unitary phenomenon. Rather canopy and undergrowth both have "closed" and "open" phases. As Napier, the originator of this approach to locomotion, pointed out, continuities and discontinuities of supports do seem to be a major factor in determining locomotion.

Support orientation and diameter cannot be looked at in isolation. They do not impose a locomotor style. Leaping and slow climbing have been shown to be equally useful in a tangle of small supports. It would be wrong, though, to take the fatalistic/relativistic view that every case is special. The support structure of a forest is limited in its diversity. Trees have their own "foraging strategy" and their own appropriate architecture. But we are a long way from being able to create many useful generalizations about habitat and activity interactions in locomotion.

We acknowledge that some of what we have done must remain tentative, in particular because of deficiencies in the data base and the difficulties of extracting information from it. On the other hand, the rather large amount of data that has been included in our studies is not paralleled, as far as we know, in any other studies of these organisms. And the analytical methods that we have used for grouping have, separately, depended upon (a) visual arrangements of the multidimensional plots of the raw data, and (b) multivariate analyses of the entire data set. Future studies will take the multivariate examination of these data much further. They will examine patterns of grouping of species in more detail, and they will also study patterns of clustering of variables and intercorrelations among both variables and species.

As an initial step to a multidimensional adaptation, we feel that this study has already produced some dividends. First, we have been able to confirm the value of a firmer level of analysis of characteristics of lifestyles. In future studies several of our variables will have to be reexamined and further subdivided. Second, "leaping" in prosimians is clearly not a unitary phenomenon, and neither is "vertical clinging." This is so whether or not the ancestral prosimian had decidedly saltatorial or/and vertical clinging tendencies.

Anatomically there seem to be at least three different kinds of leaping adaptation in prosimians (Oxnard 1983), and the results here confirm that there are three sets of lifestyles that go with them. The earlier, coarser stud-

Fig. 6.6. Comparison of the lifestyle
and anatomical arrangements of the
major groups.

Lifestyles: Niche Metrics

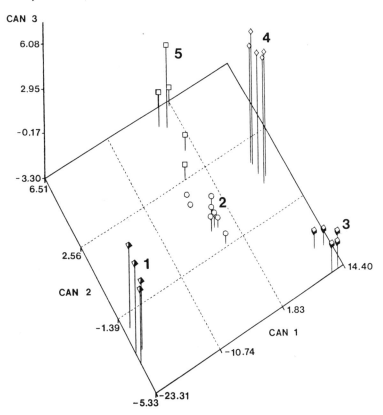

Anatomies: Morphometrics

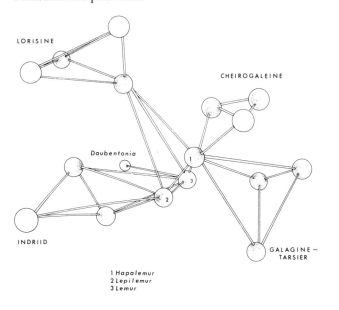

ies separated at first two groups of leaping genera—indriids and bushbaby/tarsiers (Oxnard 1973)—and later, three—(a) indriids, (b) cheirogaleines, and (c) bushbabies plus tarsiers (Oxnard 1983). But the results here perform somewhat differently. Though these new results do distinguish clearly the indriids, they add to them, unequivocally, both *Lepilemur* and *Hapalemur*. And the new results split the other two groups in a different way. The prior bushbaby/tarsier group is now seen to be a group comprising only the most extreme bushbabies (Allen's and Senegal) plus the tarsiers. And the prior cheirogaleine group is now seen to be a group of cheirogaleines plus the less extreme bushbabies. These distinctions are quite real in both the studies of lifestyles and anatomies. But they were not apparent when the animals were examined at the cruder, generic, level, and using the coarser locomotor classifications.

Galago demidovii and *Microcebus*, representing the group of bushbabies and cheirogaleines, exhibit quite frequent leaping, but show no real preference for support orientation. Viewed in a greater number of dimensions, it can be seen that they do not leap in the same way as other specialist leapers. They exhibit a clear preference for supports of small diameter, and, we believe, fill a similar niche in both canopy and undergrowth, as do the specialist slow climbers, *Arctocebus* and *Loris,* in the undergrowth alone: the "closed phase" of foliage tangles and liane curtains, respectively. But, as their diet is more generalized, so is their locomotion more versatile.

The tarsiers and, to a lesser extent, *Galago senegalensis* and *G. alleni* are filling a niche in the "open phase" of the undergrowth, just as the indriids fill a niche in the "open phase" of the canopy. But, just as they live at opposite extremes of the forest, their body size and diet lie at opposite extremes. Just as the New World prehensile-tailed species, many of the Old World langurs, and various other frugi- and folivores have often developed a degree of tension in forelimbs, so have the indriids.

The adaptations of the indriids are clear, but perhaps less distinct than those of the tarsiers from the other prosimians.

Prospect

The study has highlighted several directions in which we can go. First, more objective measures of the "distances" between species on these multiple behavioral axes and of the relative dependence or independence of variables should be attempted, no doubt using further multivariate statistical techniques.

Second, the relationship between support density, support size, support orientation, and leaping style in prosimians of various phylogenetic backgrounds and body sizes elucidates how much, if at all, our three groups have to do with each other in locomotor terms.

Third, the matter of tension-bearing behaviors in what we suspect are many different modes (perhaps as complex even as we have found leaping to be) needs further study, especially quantification. The goal is to interpolate into the current system, the several variables that it will probably generate.

Fourth, comparisons of these multidimensional lifestyle profiles have reminded us that groups are not dependent alone upon the major extreme features that animals share (for example, leaping in the various groups of leapers). Groups are often as much determined by the features that animals do not possess, or possess only in small degree, as by their shared characteristics. This is much less obviously seen in classifications that tend to speak to outstanding characteristics rather than small or missing ones. Yet these small or missing features may be very important in the biology of the situation. In the same way we have been reminded that common possession of a package of intermediate features may also be a most important defining pattern that is easily missed in the employment of a classification.

Fifth, the multidimensional lifestyle plots should be compared in detail with new multidimensional anatomical studies that include the full range of anatomies and the full range of species. This will allow us to examine fully such repeated functional correlations as may exist. These are the generalizations that we ultimately seek to produce.

The comparisons with those few anatomical (morphometric) studies that we already have available are so remarkably close as to be most encouraging. The groups determined through our lifestyle profiles have clear relationships, both in their own internal links and in their external links with the prior determined anatomical groups. The fact that the anatomical groups *were* determined before these lifestyle studies were undertaken is an especial strength in these investigations. This separation can be judged to even further increase the strength of the association when it is realized that the knowledge was kept separate in our determination of the groups. Crompton, when judging the lifestyle information, was unaware of the anatomical structure already available in certain of Oxnard's computer outputs. And these unpublished computer outputs had not, at that point, even been closely inspected by Oxnard. There was thus no chance that the lifestyle information was biased by prior knowledge of the anatomical results. The degree of concordance of the morphometrics with the lifestyle studies is greater by far than with any of the older, simpler, coarser locomotor classifications.

A final possibility is that one day we will have anatomical and lifestyle information taken in such a way that we can combine them in a single overarching statistical analysis. We cannot guess what this ultimate study (morpho-niche metrics, that is, anatomies and lifestyles combined) may show. Though the similarities presently noted between the morphometric and niche-metric analyses might make us wonder if that study would tell us anything new, we cannot complacently assume that it would not. We already have an example of what happens when larger and larger studies are added together. Who would have thought, for instance, that when morphometric studies of forelimbs and hindlimbs, which separately each provide information about function, should, when added together, provide information that seems to relate to phylogenetic relationships (Oxnard 1983).

In the meantime, the relationships that we have found are of value in helping (a) to understand the nature of the associations between lifestyles and anatomies in these living species, (b) to make predictive statements about those living species that we are unable to include in one or another of the investigations, (c) to make reverse statements about such relationships in unknown (i.e., fossil) species, and (d) to apply the same method to the remaining primates, the Anthropoidea, when equivalent field information can be obtained and synthesized. All of this then provides us with a higher level of information in ultimate evolutionary and systematic evaluations of prosimians, other primates, and other vertebrates as well.

Literature Cited

Albignac, R. 1981. "Variabilité dans l'organisation territoriale et l'écologie de *Avahi laniger.*" *Comptes Rendue Acad. Sci. Paris* 292:331–34.

Albrecht, G. H. 1980. "Multivariate analysis and the study of form, with special reference to canonical variate analysis." *Amer. Zool.* 20:679–93.

Alexander, R. McN. 1977. "Terrestrial locomotion." In *The Mechanics and Energetics of Animal Locomotion,* ed. McN. Alexander and G. Goldspink. London: Chapman Hall.

Andrews, D. F. 1972. "Plots of high-dimensional data." *Biometrics* 28:125–36.

Andrews, D. F. 1973. "Graphical techniques for high-dimensional data." In *Discriminant Analysis and Applications,* ed. T. Cacoullos, pp. 37–39. New York: Academic Press.

Ashton, E. H., and C. E. Oxnard. 1958. "Some variations of the maxillary nerve in primates." *Proc. Zool. Soc. Lond.* 131:457–70.

Ashton, E. H., and C. E. Oxnard. 1963. "The musculature of the primate shoulder." *Trans. Zool. Soc. Lond.* 29:553–650.

Ashton, E. H., and C. E. Oxnard. 1964. "Locomotor patterns in primates." *Proc. Zool. Soc. Lond.* 142:1–28.

Bearder, S. K. 1974. "Aspects of the Behaviour and Ecology of the Thick-tailed Bushbaby, *Galago crassicaudatus.*" Ph.D. dissertation, University of Witwatersrand, Johannesburg.

Bearder, S. K., and G. A. Doyle. 1974. "Ecology of bushbabies, *Galago senegalensis* and *Galago crassicaudatus,* with some notes about their behavior in the field." In *Prosimian Biology,* ed. R. D. Martin, G. A. Doyle, and A. C. Walker, pp. 109–30. London: Duckworth.

Budnitz, N., and K. Davies. 1975. "*Lemur catta*: ecology and behavior." In *Lemur Biology,* ed. I. Tattersall and R. W. Sussmann. New York: Plenum.

Campbell, B. 1937. "The shoulder musculature of the platyrrhine monkeys." *J. Mammal.* 18:293–321.

Carpenter, C. R. 1935. "A field study of the behavior and social relations of howling monkeys (*Allouatta palliata*)." *Comp. Psych. Monogr.* 10:1–168.

Charles-Dominique, P. 1977. *Ecology and Behaviour of Nocturnal Primates.* London: Duckworth.

Charles-Dominique, P., and R. D. Martin. 1970. "Evolution of lorises and lemurs." *Nature* (London) 227:257–60.

Clarke, A. B. 1978. "Sex ratio and local resource competition in a prosimian primate." *Science* 201:163–65.

Clifford, H., and W. Stephenson. 1975. *An Introduction to Numerical Classification.* New York: Academic Press.

Crompton, R. H. 1980. "Galago Locomotion." Ph.D. dissertation, Harvard University, Cambridge.

Crompton, R. H. 1983. "Age differences in locomotion of two subtropical Galaginae." *Primates* 24:241–59.

Crompton, R. H. 1984. "Foraging, habitat structure and locomotion in two subtropical Galaginae." In *Adaptations for Foraging in Primates,* ed. P. S. Rodman and J. Cant, pp. 73–111. New York: Columbia University Press.

Crompton, R. H., and P. M. Andau. 1986. "Locomotion and habitat utilization in free-ranging *Tarsius bancanus:* A preliminary report." *Primates* 27:337–55.

Crompton, R. H., and P. M. Andau. 1987. "Ranging, activity rhythms, and sociality in free-ranging *Tarsius bancanus*: A preliminary report." *Int. J. Primatol.* 8:43–71.

Dykyj, D. 1980. "Locomotion of the slow loris in a designed substrate habitat." *Amer. J. Phys. Anthro.* 52:167–82.

Elliot, O., and M. Elliot. 1967. "Field notes on the slow loris in Malaya. *J. Mammal.* 48:497–98.

Feldesman, M. R. 1976. "The primate forelimb: A morphometric study of locomotor diversity." *Univ. Oregon Anthropol. Papers* 20:440–53.

Feldesman, M. R. 1979. "Further morphometric studies of the ulna from the Omo Basin, Ethiopia." *Amer. J. Phys. Anthro.* 51:409–16.

Felsenstein, J. 1985. "Phylogenies and the comparative method." *Amer. Nat.* 125:1–15.

Fisher, R. A. 1936. "The use of multiple measurements in taxonomic problems." *Ann. Eugenics* 7:179–88.

Fleagle, J. G. 1976. "Locomotor behavior and muscular anatomy in sympatric Malaysian leafmonkeys (*Presbytis obscura* and *Presbytis melalophos*)." *Amer. J. Phys. Anthro.* 46:297–308.

Fleagle, J. G. 1979. "Primate positional behavior and anatomy: Naturalistic and experimental approaches." In *Environment, Behavior, and Morphology,* ed. M. E. Morbeck, H. Preuschoft, and N. Gomberg, pp. 313–25. New York: Fisher.

Fogden, M. 1974. "A preliminary study of the western tarsier, *Tarsius bancanus* Horsfield." In *Prosimian Biology,* ed. R. D. Martin, G. A. Doyle, and A. C. Walker. London: Duckworth.

Garber, P. A. 1984. "Use of habitat and positional behavior in a neotropical primate, *Saguinus oedipus.*" In *Adaptations for Foraging in Non-Human Primates,* ed. P. S. Rodman and J. G. H. Cant, pp. 112–33. New York: Columbia University Press.

Goodall, J. 1971. *In the Shadow of Man.* Boston: Houghton Mifflin.

Gower, J. C. 1967. "A comparison of some methods of cluster analysis." *Biometrics* 23:623–36.

Gower, J. C., and G. J. S. Ross. 1969. "Minimum spanning trees and single linkage cluster analysis." *Applied Stat. C.* 18:54–64.

Harcourt, C. S. 1980. "Behavioral Adaptations in South African Galagos." Ph.D. dissertation, University of Witwatersrand, Johannesburg.

Harrington, J. E. 1975. "Field observations of the social behavior of *Lemur fulvus fulvus.*" In *Lemur Biology,* ed. I. Tattersall and R. W. Sussman. New York: Plenum.

Hildebrand, M. 1967. "Symmetrical gaits of primates." *Amer. J. Phys. Anthro.* 26:119–30.

Hildebrand, M. 1980. "The adaptive significance of tetrapod gait selection." *Amer. Zool.* 20:225–67.

Hladik, C. M. P., P. Charles-Dominique, P. Vadebouze, J. Delart-Laval, and J. Flanzy. 1971. "La caecotrophie chez les phyllophage du genre *Lepilemur* et les correlations avec les peculiarités digestif." *Comptes Rend. Acad. Sci. Paris* 272:3191–914.

Hladik, C. M. P. and P. Charles-Dominique. 1974. "The behavior and ecology of the sportive lemur (*Lepilemur mustelinus*) in relation to its dietary peculiarities." In *Prosimian Biology,* ed. R. D. Martin et al., pp. 23–37. London: Duckworth.

Hladik, C. M. P. 1979. "Diet and ecology of prosimians." In *The Study of Prosimian Behavior,* ed. G. A. Doyle and R. D. Martin, pp. 307–55. New York: Academic Press.

Hotelling, H. 1936. "The generalization of 'students' ratio." *Ann. Math. and Stat.* 2:360–78.

Jewell, P. A., and J. F. Oates. 1969. "Ecological observations on the lorisoid primates of African lowland forest." *Zool. Africana* 4:231–48.

Jolly, A. 1966. *Lemur Biology.* Chicago: University of Chicago Press.

Jolly, A., and W. L. R. Oliver. 1985. "Predatory behavior in captive *Lemur* spp." *Zoo Biol.* 4:139–45.

Kingdon, J. 1971. *East African Mammals.* London: Academic Press.

Kinzey, W. G. 1976. "Positional behavior and ecology in *Callithrix torquatus.*" *Yrbook Phys. Anthro.* 20:468–80.

Lieberman, S. S. 1982. "The Ecology of the Leaf Litter Herpetofauna of a Neotropical Rain Forest: La Selva, Costa Rica. Ph.D. dissertation, University of Southern California.

Lieberman, S. S., R. H. Crompton, and C. E. Oxnard. 1989. "Prosimian niche metrics: A multivariate assessment." *Amer. J. Phys. Anthro.*

MacKinnon, J. and K. MacKinnon. 1980. "The behavior of wild spectral tarsiers." *Int. J. Primatol.* 1:4–16.

McArdle, J. E. 1978. "The Functional Morphology of the Hip and Thigh of the Lorisiformes." Ph.D. dissertation, University of Chicago.

McArdle, J. E. 1981. *Functional Morphology of the Hip and Thigh of the Lorisiformes.* Basel: Karger.

Mahalanobis, P. C. 1936. "On the generalized distance in statistics." *Proc. Nat. Inst. Sci. India* 2:49–55.

Manaster, B. J. M. 1976. "Locomotor Adaptations within the *Cercopithecus, Cercocebus,* and *Presbytis* Genera." Ph.D. dissertation, University of Chicago.

Martin, R. D. 1972. "A preliminary study of the lesser mouse lemur (*Microcebus murinus* J. F. Miller 1777). *Zeit. Comp. Ethol. Suppl.* 9:43–89.

Mittermeier, R. A. 1978. "Locomotion and posture in *Ateles geoffroyi* and *Ateles paniscus.*" *Folia Primatol.* 30:161–93.

Mollison, T. 1910. "Die Korperproportionen der Primaten." *Morph. Jahrb.* 42:79–304.

Morbeck, M. E. 1979. "Forelimb use and positional adaptation in *Colobus guereza:* Integration of behavioral, ecological, and anatomical data." In *Environment, Behavior and Morphology: Dynamic Interactions in Primates,* ed. M. E. Morbeck, H. Preuschoft, and N. Gomberg, pp. 95–118. New York: Fischer.

Napier, J. R., and P. Davis. 1959. "The forelimb skeleton and associated remains of *Proconsul africanus.*" *Fossil Mammals of Africa,* No. 16, pp. 1–69. London: British Museum of Natural History.

Napier, J. R., and P. H. Napier. 1967. *A Handbook of the Living Primates.* London: Academic Press.

Napier, J. R., and P. H. Napier. 1985. *The Living Primates.* London: Academic Press.

Napier, J. R., and A. C. Walker. 1967. "Vertical clinging and leaping: A newly recognized category of locomotor behaviour of primates." *Folia Primatol.* 21:250–76.

Nash, L. 1983. "Differential habitat utilization in two species of sympatric galago in Kenya. *Amer. J. Phys. Anthro.* 60:231.

Niemitz, C. 1979. "Outline of the behavior of *Tarsius bancanus.*" In *The Study of Prosimian Behavior,* ed. G. A. Doyle and R. D. Martin. New York: Academic Press.

Niemitz, C. 1983. "New results on the locomotion of *Tarsius bancanus* Horsfield, 1821. *Ann. Sci. Nat. Zool. Paris* 13:89–100.

Niemitz, C. 1984a. "Synecological relationships and feeding behavior of the genus *Tarsius.* In *The Biology of Tarsiers,* ed. C. Niemitz, pp. 59–76. Stuttgart: Fischer.

Niemitz, C. 1984b. "Activity rhythms and use of space in semi-wild Bornean tarsiers, with remarks on the wild spectral tarsier." In *The Biology of Tarsiers,* ed. C. Niemitz, pp. 85–116. Stuttgart: Fischer.

Oates, J. H. 1984. "The niche of the potto, *Perodicticus potto. Int. J. Primatol.* 5:21–61.

Oxnard, C. E. 1967. "The functional morphology of the primate shoulder as revealed by comparative anatomical, osteometric and discriminant function techniques." *Amer. J. Phys. Anthro.* 26:219–40.

Oxnard, C. E. 1969. "The combined use of multivariate and clustering analyses in functional morphology." *J. Biomech.* 2:73–88.

Oxnard, C. E. 1972. "Functional morphology of primates: Some mathematical and physical methods." In *The Functional and Evolutionary Biology of Primates*, ed. R. H. Tuttle, pp. 305–36. Chicago: Aldine-Atherton.

Oxnard, C. E. 1973. "Some locomotor adaptations among lower primates." *Symp. Zool. Soc. Lond.* 33:255–99.

Oxnard, C. E. 1975. "Primate locomotor classifications for evaluating fossils: Their inutility, and an alternative." *Proc. Symp. Fifth Congr. Internat. Primatol. Soc.* 5:269–84.

Oxnard, C. E. 1981. "The uniqueness of *Daubentonia*." *Amer. J. Phys. Anthro.* 83:1–22.

Oxnard, C. E. 1983. *The Order of Man: A Biomathematical Anatomy of the Primates*. Hong Kong: Hong Kong University Press. First published in the United States by Yale University Press in 1984.

Oxnard, C. E. 1987. *Fossils, Teeth and Sex: New Perspectives on Human Evolution*. Hong Kong: Hong Kong University Press; Seattle and London: University of Washington Press.

Oxnard, C. E., R. Z. German, F-K. Jouffroy, and J. Lessertisseur. 1981. "The morphometrics of limb proportions in leaping prosimians." *Amer. J. Phys. Anthro.* 54:421–30.

Oxnard, C. E., R. Z. German, and J. E. McArdle. 1981. "The functional morphometrics of the hip and thigh in leaping prosimians." *Amer. J. Phys. Anthro.* 54:481–98.

Oxnard, C. E., and P. Neely. 1969. "The descriptive use of neighborhood limited classification in functional morphology: An analysis of the shoulder in primates." *J. Morph.* 129:117–48.

Pagés, E. 1978. "Home range, behaviour and tactile communication in a nocturnal Malagasy lemur, *Microcebus coquereli*. In *Recent Advances in Primatology*, ed. D. Chivers and J. Herbert. London: Academic Press.

Petter, J. J. 1962. Recherches sur l'écologie et l'éthologie des lémuriens malgaches. *Mem. Mus. d'Hist. Nat.* 27:1–146.

Petter, J. J., and C. M. Hladik. 1970. "Observations sur la domaine vital et la densité de population de *Loris tardigradus* (Linnaeus). *J. Bombay Nat. Hist. Soc.* 54:387–98.

Petter, J. J., and A. Peyreiras. 1970a. "Nouvelle contribution a l'étude d'un lémurien Malgache, le Aye-Aye (*Daubentonia madagascariensis* E. Geoffroy). *Mammalia* 34:169–93.

Petter, J. J., and A. Peyriéras. 1970b. "Observations éco-éthologiques sur les lémuriens Malgache du genre *Hapalemur*. *Terre et Vie* 24:356–82.

Petter, J. J., and A. Peyriéras. 1974. "A study of the population density and home range of *Indri indri* in Madagascar." In *Prosimian Biology*, ed. R. D. Martin, G. A. Doyle, and A. C. Walker. London: Duckworth.

Petter, J. J., and A. Peyriéras. 1975. "Preliminary notes on the behaviour and ecology of *Hapalemur griseus*. In *Lemur Biology*, ed. I. Tattersall and R. W. Sussman. New York: Plenum.

Petter, J. J., A. Schilling, and G. Pariente. 1971. "Observations éco-éthologiques sur deux lémuriens Malgache nocturnes: *Phaner furcifer* et *Microcebus coquereli*." *Terre et Vie* 25:287–327.

Petter, J. J., A. Schilling, and G. Pariente. 1975. "Observations on the behaviour and ecology of *Phaner furcifer*." In *Lemur Biology*, ed. I. Tattersall and R. W. Sussman. New York: Plenum.

Pollock, J. I. 1975a. "The Social Behavior and Ecology of *Indri indri*." Ph.D. dissertation, University of London.

Pollock, J. I. 1975b. "Field observations on *Indri indri*, a preliminary report." In *Lemur Biology*, ed. I. Tattersall and R. W. Sussman. New York: Plenum.

Pollock, J. I. 1977. "The ecology and sociology of feeding in *Indri indri*." In *Primate Ecology*, ed. T. Clutton-Brock, pp. 37–69. London: Academic Press.

Pollock, J. I. 1979. "Spatial distribution and ranging behavior in lemurs. In *The Study of Prosimian Behavior*, ed. G. A. Doyle and R. D. Martin, pp. 359–407. New York: Academic Press.

Priemel, G. 1937. "Die platyrrhinen Affen als Bewegungstype unter besondere Berucksichtigung der Extremformen *Callicebus* und *Ateles*." *Zeit. Morph. Okolog. Tiere* 33:1–52.

Prost, J. H. 1967. "A definitional system for the classification of primate locomotion." *Am. J. Phys. Anthro.* 26:149–70.

Redford, K. H., G. A. Bouchardet da Fonseca, and T. E. Lacher. "The relationship between frugivory and insectivory in primates." *Primates* 25:433–40.

Richard, A. F. 1974. "Patterns of mating in *Propithecus verreauxi verreauxi*." In *Prosimian Biology*, ed. R. D. Martin, G. A. Doyle, and A. C. Walker. London: Duckworth.

Richard, A. F. 1977. "The feeding behaviour of *Propithecus verreauxi*." In *Primate Ecology: Studies of Feeding and Ranging Behaviors in Lemurs, Monkeys, and Apes*, ed. T. H. Clutton-Brock. London: Academic Press.

Ripley, S. 1967. "The leaping of langurs, a problem in the study of locomotor adaptation." *Amer. J. Phys. Anthro.* 26:149–70.

Rodman, P. S. 1979. "Skeletal differentiation of *Macaca fascicularis* and *Macaca nemestrina* in relation to arboreal and terrestrial quadrupedalism." *Amer. J. Phys. Anthrop.* 51:51–62.

Rodman, P. S., and J. Cant. 1984. *Adaptations for Foraging in Primates*. New York: Columbia.

Rollinson, J., and R. D. Martin. 1980. "Comparative aspects of primate locomotion, with special reference to arboreal cercopithecines." *Symp. Zool. Soc. Lond.* 48:377–427.

Rose, M. D. 1973. "Quadrupedalism in Primates." *Primates* 4:337–57.

Rose, M. D. 1974. "Postural adaptations in New and Old World monkeys." In *Primate Locomotion*, ed. F. Jenkins. New York: Academic Press.

Russell, R. 1977. "The Behavior, Ecology and Environmental Physiology of a Nocturnal Primate, *Lepilemur mustelinus*." Ph.D. dissertation, Duke University.

Sprankel, H. 1965. "Untersuchungen an *Tarsius*. I. Morphologie des Schwanzes nebst Ethologischen Bermerkungen." *Folia Primatol.* 3:153–88.

Stern, J. T., Jr., and C. E. Oxnard. 1973. *Primate Locomotion: Some Links with Evolution and Morphology*. Basel: Karger.

Subramoniam, S. 1957. "Some observations on the habits of the slender loris, *Loris tardigradus* (Linnaeus)." *J. Bombay Nat. Hist. Soc.* 54:387–98.

Sussman, R. W. 1974. "Ecological distinctions in sympatric species of *Lemur*." In *Prosimian Biology*, ed. R. D. Martin, G. A. Doyle, and A. C. Walker. London: Duckworth.

Sussman, R. W., and I. Tattersall. 1975. "Observations on the ecology and behavior of the mongoose lemur, *Lemur mongoz mongoz* Linnaeus (Primates, Lemuriformes) at Ampijoroa, Madagascar." *Anthrop. Papers Amer. Mus. Nat. Hist.* 52:193–216.

Tattersall, I. 1977. "Ecology and behavior of *Lemur fulvus mayottensis* (Primates, Lemuriformes)." *Anthrop. Papers Amer. Mus. Nat. Hist.* 54:421–82.

Tattersall, I. 1982. *The Primates of Madagascar*. New York: Columbia University Press.

Taylor, C. R., K. Schmidt-Nielsen, and J. C. Raab. 1970. "Scaling of energetic cost of locomotion to body size in mammals." *Amer. J. Physiol.* 219:1104–07.

Walker, A. C. 1969. "The locomotion of the lorises, with special relation to the potto." *E. Afr. Wildlife J.* 7:1–5.

Walker, A. C. 1974. "Locomotor adaptations in past and present prosimian primates." In *Primate Locomotion*, ed. F. Jenkins. New York: Academic Press.

Walker, A. C. 1979. "Prosimian locomotor behavior." In *The Study of Primate Behaviour*, ed. G. A. Doyle and R. D. Martin. London: Duckworth.

Zuckerman, S., E. H. Ashton, R. M. Flinn, C. E. Oxnard, and T. F. Spence. 1973. "Some locomotor features of the pelvic girdle in primates." *Symp. Zool. Soc. Lond.* 33:71–165.

Index